A RAINBOW IN THE SKY

By the same Author

✻

ROWING
(*with* Dr. P. C. Mallam)

Editor and Contributor to
LIFE'S A PUDDING
(Autobiography of the late Guy Nickalls)
and
WITH THE SKIN OF THEIR TEETH

'Disagreeable Me'. A self portrait. *c.* 1935

A Rainbow in the Sky

REMINISCENCES

By

G. O. (Gully) Nickalls

My heart leaps up when I behold
A rainbow in the sky

WILLIAM WORDSWORTH

1974
CHATTO & WINDUS
LONDON

Published by
Chatto & Windus Ltd
40 William IV Street
London W.C.2 N 4DF

*

Clarke, Irwin & Co. Ltd
Toronto

All rights reserved. No part of this publication may be reproduced, stored in a retrieval system, or transmitted in any form, or by any means, electronic, mechanical, photocopying, recording or otherwise, without the prior permission of Chatto & Windus Ltd.

ISBN 0 7011 2069 X

© G. O. Nickalls 1974

Printed in Great Britain
by Ebenezer Baylis & Son Ltd
The Trinity Press, Worcester, and London

For my wife, Rachel,
who has allowed me to complete this book
with the minimum of interference.

AUTHOR'S NOTE

I have much pleasure in thanking a number of people who have helped in the production of this book. I have throughout been extremely fortunate in having the assistance of Joanna Scott-Moncrieff who advised on certain omissions and rearranged portions of the text to make a far more cohesive whole.

I am greatly indebted to my dear cousin "Moggs" for the patient and cheerful way in which she typed and retyped my original manuscripts.

My thanks are also due to the Right Reverend Gerald Ellison, the Bishop of London, in establishing the fact that the headgear worn by one of his predecessors (in the chapter headed "Three Characters in Search of an Author") was, in fact, a Canterbury cap.

It was as generous of the proprietors of *The Queen* to allow me to reproduce "You Should Have Seen us Dance the Polka", a chapter which originally appeared in their journal, as it was of *The Courier* magazine who authorised the reprinting of my verses on Delphi and lines descriptive of Henley Regatta.

Finally, I would like to thank Mrs. George Bambridge and Eyre Methuen Ltd. for their permission to quote from Rudyard Kipling's poem, "When Earth's Last Picture Is Painted".

CONTENTS

Chapter		page
1	I Start Showing Off	9
2	"You Should Have Seen us Dance the Polka"	17
3	Sex Rears Its Beautiful Head	23
4	The Happiest Years of My Life?	34
5	Pierrots In Uniform	48
6	Hunting In No-Man's-Land	56
7	Home Sweet Home?	72
8	No, No, They Can't Take That Away From Me	78
9	"Ship Money, You Bloody Fool!"	84
10	Across The Herring Pond	94
11	Unemployed! Unemployable?	107
12	I Deserve To Be Hung	119
13	Three Characters In Search of an Author	125
14	I Get That Sinking Feeling	139
15	From Megaphones to Microphones	151
16	All At Sea	161
17	"Please to Stop the Shooting"	170
18	Wigs, Gowns and Tow-ropes	177
19	A Peep Behind the "Iron Curtain"	183
	Postscript	190

ILLUSTRATIONS

"Disagreeable Me." A Self Portrait *c.* 1935   *Frontispiece*

A "kill" in No-Man's Land   *facing page* 64
G. O. Nickalls bow and steers with R. S. C. Lucas

Our wedding, November 5, 1929   65
The Oxford crew at my parents' house, 1923

My mother with her youngest son, Rodney   80
The author in rowing kit, 1921

Henley Regatta, Finals   81
Oxford and Cambridge Boat Race

University Boat Race, 1949; Umpire G. O. Nickalls   152
Count F. Van den Heuvel with the author

The Oxford Connection   153

Chapter 1

I Start Showing Off

I WAS just six years old when I became conscious of my father's fame in the rowing world. For it was then that I was first taken to Henley Regatta and told that I was to be allowed on the Umpire's launch "to watch Daddy row", that I would see him at the start but that I was not to try to speak to him nor was I to shout or clap or make any noise whatsoever. I remember it so well. I was sitting in the bow of the launch and as my father was backing down his pair-oar to get the stern of the boat on to the starting punt, he glanced up and winked at me. My heart was very full and a thrill of pride surged through me. That god-like creature had seen me and, oh joy, he had winked at me. What more had life to offer? I was hooked.

Admittedly my very first years on this planet had been passed in the most excruciating boredom. Nothing but walks, walks, walks. A walk in the morning and then another walk in the afternoon, followed by a brief presentation to our parents after tea — how well we came to know the lanes around Farnham Royal where we grew up. As soon as we could be relied upon not to interrupt the proceedings we were taken to church on Sunday morning and this came as a distinct relief to the seemingly interminable weekday routine of perambulation upon perambulation.

My young brother's pram was of the limousine type familiar in the present day; but, as soon as I was old enough to sit upright, I was promoted to a two-wheeler built of cane and wicker-work which gave it a somewhat bizarre, rickshaw appearance. Nanny was in charge of the limousine, while the under-nurse, a darling girl called Bessie, pushed or pulled me about in the rickshaw. This was the invariable rule except when the road ran uphill. At this point I was commanded to dismount, the limousine was turned round and I was ordered to stretch out my arms behind me, take hold of the rail or handlebar and pull the limousine up the incline while Nanny did some token pushing in the region of the hood. This I was told was good for me. (When one is young everything in the least bit unpleasant is good for one. Pulling prams uphill was certainly good for one. It improved your carriage and prevented the development of rounded shoulders.) Just how boring were those walks can be gauged by a clear remembrance of the very few things that we encountered on our travels. A tree uprooted by a storm overnight was an awesome sight, meriting at least five minutes close inspection. A runaway horse or a pair of runaway horses engendered the most tremendous excitement. Sometimes an unoccupied carriage or trap swayed and tottered in a most fearsome manner in the wake of the steeds; on other occasions a pair of broken shafts hard on their heels dragged a perilous and clattering course along the highway.

Could life hold more excitement? Sometimes we would pass a coloured gentleman or as we termed him a "blackamoor". It was only on the rarest occasions we would meet a Chinaman complete with the well-groomed pigtail they wore in those days. Beyond those red letter days nothing, nothing whatsoever ever happened.

The character of my second Nanny, good woman though she was, was inclined to be on the tough side. She was the offspring of a policeman at Didcot and a firm believer in discipline, law and order. I think you would call her a religious woman, especially should your ideas on religion tend towards the hell fire and eternal damnation variety. As a family we were regular churchgoers. On one occasion when my father shirked what she considered his obvious duty, Nanny told us God would punish him. "How?" we asked. "He will send the birds to eat up all the seeds he's planted in the garden." In my view my father got off pretty lightly.

Nanny's religious instruction had its positive side. As a temporary relaxation from pram-pushing she would, during

I START SHOWING OFF

one of those interminable walks, seat herself on a tree trunk or a five bar gate. She would produce an apple and with horse-like teeth bite off large chunks and distribute one piece to my brother and another to myself. I am bound to admit that this form of distribution never really appealed to my elementary views on hygiene. It was however better than nothing. After the apple distribution she would produce a prayer book from her pocket and by continual repetition I learned the catechism by heart. I became word perfect, which saved me the bother of learning it when I eventually proceeded to school. I had little notion of its meaning and I doubt if she had either, and I am still uncertain as to why my name was "N or M". However, with my catechism buttoned up to the last syllable we moved on to the *Venite*, the *Te Deum* and the *Nunc Dimittis*.

As soon as we were old enough, my parents took us to Matins every Sunday morning. Those with any experiences of church services will know that on the entrance of the parson and the choir the congregation rises—a form of reverential salutation which has always seemed to me to be very right and proper. My mother, my brother and myself conformed to this custom. Not so my father, who with arms defiantly akimbo remained firmly seated. I never got over the ghastly embarrassment of my father's inactivity on these occasions. I never knew the reason for it. Apparently it had something to do with his Quaker forebears. If, on occasions, you remained seated in God's house, why should you rise on the entrance of his servant, the parson? His mother had told him that such a practice was sheer idolatry; I never comprehended this reasoning. In fact the whole thing made me feel so thoroughly uncomfortable that I never ever mentioned the subject.

As soon as I could read, my mother was wont to invite me to render certain passages from suitable books to any assembled company. I obliged readily, and my mother obviously thought that I was the only child ever to have mastered this particular accomplishment. Nowadays I am quite horrified at the memory of the unadulterated readings which tripped happily from my tongue. Even now I recall one sentence — "the whale is a mammal which gives suck to its young".

In fact I was well on the way to becoming a ghastly little show-off — a tendency which, I fear, has never entirely left me; and it certainly did not escape the attention of the terrifying being who ruled our nursery. For at least an hour, on one of our walks, I was lectured in no uncertain terms on the deadly sin of showing off. How unfunny it was! I cannot believe that many children can have been made to feel more worm-like. Tears of shame dampened my pillow as vainly I sought solace in sleep. I was relieved when I had learned to ride a bike and on occasions could accompany my mother on shopping expeditions. I was still very young but I found it all so exhilarating that ten miles in a morning induced no sort of fatigue. But a new form of showing off now reared its ugly head. My mother was determined that I should learn some pieces for recitation. The first I can recall was about a small boy who gave way to various temptations. On one occasion he secretly gorged himself on strawberry jam. As he got into bed that night his conscience pricked him and he heard the owl hoot "'T was you". "'T was you". The exact intonation of the owl hooting "'T was you" merited a good deal of careful rehearsal as we pedalled our way towards Slough one sunny morning. But there was more, much more to follow.

A few years back I was sometimes entertained by an ancient and revered uncle. He was one of the old school in the widest sense of that overworked term. That anything should be indulged in or enjoyed without a chastening period of pain and suffering was to him not only a modern namby-pamby concept, but unhealthy and slightly indecent. And so it was that whenever the future of some young man came under discussion, he would raise his eyebrows, his cold blue eyes would open wide and stare unseeingly in front of him. This seemed to indicate not so much any particular lucid recollections of the lad, as sheer and utter astonishment that such a being existed at all. He would then, throwing back his head and gazing contemplatively towards the ceiling, inquire, "And how old might he be now?" On being told that the boy might be rising fourteen, he would lower his glance, his eyebrows would drop Skye-terrier-like over his orbs, and in a tone of voice measured, foreboding and slightly sadistic, he would ask, "Have they put him to shooting yet?"

It was obvious that, in Uncle's estimation, shooting was not something you took up of your own free will, nor approached lightly or wantonly. As in the training of retrievers, it was something the victim was "put to": something in which the enjoyment of the sport played no part, and that could be attained only through tedious, purgatorial correction, over a long period of time.

It was not, however, in a spirit of sadism, but rather in a spirit of maternal exhibitionism, that at the tender age of five I was "put to" reciting.

Now recitation occupied a particularly cosy corner in the hearts of the late Victorians and the Edwardians. I couldn't sing, and solo dancing, though fit and proper for girls, was considered a little unmanly for boys. Recitation was therefore the *métier* chosen for me. In a few months' time there was to be a concert at Cookham. Performers were to be confined to children—anything from toddlers to teenagers. My Aunt Emily was already coaching her Harry for his particular role. This put my mother on her mettle, and there was to be no time lost. Two pieces were selected for me: "The Chinaman", by Thackeray, and a little rhyme entitled "Mrs. Skinner". Of the two, "The Chinaman" was by far the harder nut to crack.

"Now," said my mother at the first rehearsal, "the first thing you do is to walk confidently down to the front of the stage, give the title of the piece and its author." Sheepishly I advanced across the room and in a dull, toneless voice announced: "'The Chinaman', by William Makepeeth Fackerwee." "No, no, no!" cried my mother. "Say it as though you were going to give the audience a special treat. Say it as though you were interested in it. For if you're not interested in it, nobody else will be. It's a pity that you lisp. But no doubt you will grow out of it when you get older." We continued with the first verse:

A RAINBOW IN THE SKY
There lived a sage in days of yore
And he a handsome pigtail wore —

"Get hold of the pigtail from behind your back," coached my mother, "and hold it at arm's length to one side. You see, the audience doesn't yet know you've got a pigtail. You must establish the pigtail" . . . I continued:

But wondered much and sorrowed more,
Because it hung behind him.

"You can throw your pigtail back over your shoulder at that point, darling." The second verse loomed in front of me:

He mused upon this curious case —

"Oliver, you know how people muse. Hold up the forefinger of your right hand, like this. . . . Now put it underneath your chin, with your head slightly on one side. That's right."

He mused upon this curious case,
And swore he'd change the pigtail's place —

"I think you could do an angry little stamp just before the word 'swore'. Mind, *before* 'swore', not after. That's what's known as timing." Doggedly I repeated:

And (stamp) swore he'd change the pigtail's place
And have it dangling at his face;
Not dangling there behind him.

"I think on these last two lines, darling, you could give them just one more glimpse of the pigtail. You see, they've probably forgotten all about it by now." As the wretched thing in all its sleek, snaky horror had been revealed to them only fifteen seconds before, it seemed to me almost incredible that their recollection could be so short.

The next two stanzas were devoted entirely to the mad whirlwind-like gyrations of this lunatic Chinaman to get the pigtail hanging down over his face. Frantically I jumped and

I START SHOWING OFF

pranced round the stage in futile efforts to accomplish the impossible. At last I had to own I was beaten, and for the last verse, as my mother expressed it: "More in sorrow than in anger, you drop right down into a minor key."

> Although his efforts never slack,
> Although he twist and turn and tack,
> Alas, still faithful to his back,
> The pigtail hangs behind him.

"Turn right round, show your back to the audience. They'll want to see the pigtail once more. Turn round again, bow, and wait for the curtain!" shouted my mother, as though her voice were in imminent danger of being drowned by the thunderous applause which she already heard acknowledging the histrionic precocity of her little one.

I suppose it was at Brighton, where she was at school, that my mother acquired her histrionic ambitions and she was inclined to remind us that at her particular academy they had been taught by Mr. Pertwee who, on several occasions, had told her that she possessed "very good elocution". Some years back I asked Roland Pertwee, whose play "Pink String and Sealing Wax" was set in Brighton and had just finished a successful West End run, whether his father had instructed the young ladies of the Brighton seminaries. "Yes," he said, "and I've never known any girl who, after my father's coaching, had not gone out into the world convinced that she was a budding Sarah Bernhardt." So it was that I became a victim of this blind, child-like faith engendered by Mr. Pertwee.

Perhaps favourite of all my efforts at recitation was the gruesome and poignant story of the little boy — or was it a girl — who was trampled to death by prancing steeds drawing a Victorian carriage. My mother in later years used to burlesque the piece yet, even so, she caused her sister-in-law to burst into uncontrollable sobs which completely broke up a Christmas party.

The first two verses are written in childish dialect:

A RAINBOW IN THE SKY

"Witing letters, is 'ooo Mama?
Cant I wite a letter too?"
"No, no darling, Mama busy:
Run and play with Kitty now."
"No, no Mama, me wite letters;
Tan if 'oo will show me how."
And a stamp in sport I placed it
On the little darling's brow.

The child in ecstasy rushes out of the house, disguised as a message for Papa; "prancing steeds"—the inevitable happens, and then: "reverently they raised my darling, brushed aside the locks of gold." And finally: "Mama's message was with Dod" . . .

Mind you, these excerpts are all quoted from memory after a gap of well over sixty years. I cannot vouch for their authenticity, word for word. The Victorians, I suppose, had wallowed in these recitals, which then had little competition. No all pervading screen stars stole our thunder—no thrusting TV personalities filched our public. Down in the country, we amateurs had it all our own way; and didn't we make the most of it?

Chapter 2

"You Should Have Seen us Dance the Polka"

ANOTHER essential accomplishment in the eyes of my mother was the ability to dance. Every Wednesday afternoon, chaperoned by our mothers, governesses or nannies, we were bundled into a brougham, a trap or a brake and driven to a suitable venue, sometimes to the Carr Gomm's at Farnham Royal and at others to the Slough Town Hall.

On arrival, we were herded into the dancing teacher's presence and as we assembled on the floor the mothers would take up their position on a row of chairs on one side of the room; the opposite side being occupied by a cluster of governesses and, at a respectful distance, a handful of nannies. These positions were religiously maintained, except when one of the governesses graciously deigned to patronize a nanny, or, greatly daring, would cross the floor to explain to one of the mothers that little Helen's absence was due to "the croup", and what with that succession of steaming kettles carried up three flights of stairs at all hours of the day and night, what a time they had all had with her....

Meanwhile the pianist struck a chord. "All take your partners," commanded Miss Pope, and then with a "One, two, three," we pranced off into a jolly little polka. The mothers, sitting in a row like a party of benign and broody owls, conversed in tones which in moments of excessive animation percolated through the treble of the piano and the rhythmic patter of little feet. "Miss Pope, of course, is a wonderful teacher," they said. "And so she should be. After all she was a pupil of Miss Wordsworth's." The exact identity of Miss Wordsworth was never revealed to me. In their eyes, however, she was the godhead of terpsichorean art, with Miss Pope as her favourite archangel. At any rate, they were getting their money's worth.

Through her gold spectacles Miss Pope kept an eagle eye on her class. With her hair scraped up in a neat topknot, she wore a tight-fitting black or dark brown silk dress, relieved on occasions by an oh-so-discreet floral pattern. Her neck was encased in a lace jabot, with frills which fell like a well-disciplined waterfall from above her throat to the apex of her ample yet strictly controlled bosom. The lace motif was repeated at the wrists. One seldom saw her shoes, except a momentary glance as of two shy and scurrying black mice.

For the greater part of the time she glided and gyrated with no apparent support other than that provided by the skirt itself. Sometimes, to demonstrate some point of technique, she would draw back the hem of her skirt and half reveal the pointed noses of the little black mice, which in a moment or two her correction completed, would return demurely to their inner sanctum.

But now, with a clap of her hands, the piano faltered into silence, and the class halted agog. With a bony, beckoning forefinger, Miss Pope would command, "That little boy over there. Come here!" Obediently yet sheepishly the boy approached the presence. "Little boy, you're dancing as though you were frightened of falling down. Now, if I fell down I've got twice as far to fall as you have, yet I'm not frightened of falling down. So don't dance as though you were afraid." At that moment, looking up at that formidable figure, it must have seemed to the embarrassed child that Miss Pope would have to fall at least three or four times as far before she ended flat on the ground, and wouldn't that serve her jolly well right.

On special occasions, to inject new life and interest into the class, Miss Pope would produce an exhibition pupil (a sort of demonstration model) who would emerge from behind a screen complete in ballet skirt, with little pink bows gathering in her daringly short puff sleeves. With her blonde hair, her pretty yet hard little face, and her assertive self-composure, I found her thrilling yet terrifying—the epitome of the unattainable.

"YOU SHOULD HAVE SEEN US DANCE THE POLKA"

Taking up her position a pace or so in front, yet slightly to one side, of this apparition, Miss Pope, with a peremptory nod to the pianist, would proceed to show off her pupil as though she were some performing animal. Between the first two fingers of her right hand, she held a small lace-edged handkerchief, with her little finger crooked as though over a genteel cup of tea; the other hand was used to wave a certain timing and rhythm into the pianist.

"One, two, three, four, dainty little Ve-ve, dainty little Ve-ve," and as Miss Pope glided and cavorted in front, Ve-ve would mime, scrape and point her toes in time to the music. "Now to the right, dear, dainty little Ve-ve, now to the left, dainty, dainty little Ve-ve," until with a final flourish and a low curtsey Ve-ve would be lost for ever from our view behind that tantalizing screen.

Encouraged, no doubt, by this stirring display, my mother decided to produce an exhibition pupil of her own, and I was to be the victim of her fell designs. Miss Pope announced that the following week we were to learn what my mother termed "the corkscrew", though obviously there was some technical term for it. Briefly, it is a motion which by turning the foot and shin inwards, carrying them outwards, backwards and then forwards, a fetching flourish is given to a carefully pointed toe — first with the right foot, and then with the left. My mother, who had had dancing lessons in her youth, could give a very creditable rendering of an Irish jig at the age of sixty. At family gatherings and on special festive occasions, with a spirit which belied her years, she would oblige with excerpts. As, however, on these occasions, in addition to dancing she insisted on providing her own vocal accompaniment, it is hardly surprising that the excerpts were of brief duration, and when she refused an encore she was probably entirely right in her protestation that she really shouldn't go on, "as it is so bad for my heart".

For one whole week we worked at "the corkscrew" one hour every evening. My mother would lift her skirts and demonstrate the movements with amazing dexterity, coaching and cajoling the clumsiness from my nether limbs until I had attained her own high standard. And then the moment arrived. Not a word to anyone, of course. I was put in the back row, and after an explanation of the movements Miss Pope called on the pianist, and with the usual "One, two, three" we were off. Hardly had I executed two "corkscrews" than Miss Pope, with a clap of her hands, brought the class to a standstill. "There's a boy in the back row there doing this quite perfectly. Oliver, come up here, face the class, and show them how to do it. Now, children, don't try to do anything yourselves; just watch Oliver." So once again, this time all alone, with a terrifying and repulsive smugness, I plunged into the "corkscrew" routine. I had become, if only for a few minutes, the demonstration pupil. My mother's triumph was complete. It was not long before her elder brothers heard all about it, not to mention one of her elder sisters who had a son a few months younger than I was. Her only retort was that she had taken Harry to *his* dancing class at Bourne End, and out of the blue another mother, pointing to Harry, had asked, "Do tell me, who is that extremely intelligent-looking child?"

These gyrations were not half as embarrassing as those I endured at my private school a few years later. There, when dancing class was announced, we, for some inexplicable reason, rushed up to our dormitories, donned our white flannel cricketing blazers, slipped on our patent leather dancing shoes and stretching our white kid gloves on to our hands as we descended the stairs, presented ourselves to the pale-eyed dancing master, Mr. Gautier—an awe-inspiring figure with a bald head and luxuriant drooping moustachios. His pince-nez remained *in situ* throughout the most strenuous dances. Resplendent in a black frock coat, he would, whilst buttoning on his own white kid gloves, bid us take our partners for the first dance, which was the Berlin Polka. No girls were present and I invariably felt a certain shame in requesting some mite for the pleasure of a Berlin Polka. The usual arguments ensued. "I don't mind dancing the Berlin Polka with Jefferson, so long as I can have the barn dance with Cooksey." For Cooksey excelled at the barn dance. At last we were all sorted out, and proceeded to

"YOU SHOULD HAVE SEEN US DANCE THE POLKA"

prance round the room to the strains of "Top of the morning, Billy McGee. Top of the morning, Billy McGaw". This performance never came up to my father's experience as a small boy, when his dancing master not only instructed but provided his own fiddle accompaniment as he galloped about in his carpet slippers.

By the time Christmas came round, the Edwardian child was supposed to have been suitably groomed for the ballroom. Then came the round of children's dances. There were plenty of these in the neighbourhood. The Williams' annual affair was usually rated the gayest and the best. Protesting violently that we didn't want to go, we were packed off to their house at Burnham, as often as not with our rector's family — Helen, Queenie, and their younger brother, Frederick Wilder. My Nanny often suggested I should marry Queenie. "You may think Helen the prettier," she would say. "But, mark my words, Queenie is the good-tempered one."

Frederick was known as "Monkey Bobs" — "Monkey Bobs Wilder" — and he had invented the name for himself. At the tender age of four he had announced to an astonished family that he no longer wished to be called Frederick; henceforth "Monkey Bobs" was his real name. Who could deny any child with so lively and original a mind such a reasonable request? Arrived at the party, Monkey Bobs would enter the ballroom, and, taking a short yet determined run, would slide from one end of the floor to the other. Walking back to his group of admirers clustered around the door, he would, like a cricket captain who had inspected the pitch and found it to his liking, announce that the floor was excellent. I don't think he ever danced. Usually he was busy sampling the ices at the refreshment counter. Now and then, between dances, he would return to the ballroom, test the floor again, express his approval or, feeling it getting a bit sticky, would advise the sprinkling of a little more French chalk.

Those were the days of the Swedish Dance. This was a sophisticated form of the "Oranges and Lemons" nursery game. It consisted of shunting your partner backwards and forwards, running under archways of uplifted arms, dropping on to one knee, and clapping, and all sorts of other exciting motions. Then there was the invariable chaos caused by our failing to remember the second — or was it the third? — movement of the Lancers. Sir Roger de Coverley was a great favourite. Galloping down between the lines to greet the little girl from the opposite end, and twirl her around, first with the right hand, then with the left, then with both hands — this preceded by a hissed admonition from some parent, "Now, Oliver, don't be too rough with little Betty. Remember, she isn't made the same as you." Finally, with our hands on our hips we encircled each other back to back, the weary pianist not daring to stop till each child had had its turn.

Writ large on my memory are the fabulous fancy dress parties the Desboroughs gave at Taplow Court. The first time I went as a chef. Somehow I never got into the skin of the part, refusing to dance until some kind boy lent me his golliwog mask, which banished my self-consciousness and emboldened me to take the floor without a qualm.

The following year I recall Monica Grenfell (the late Lady Salmond) utterly enchanting as a Bacchante, with her elder brothers Julian and Billy god-like in chain armour. What a long time ago it all seems. What a long time ago it was — sixty five years — and what fun we had.

Chapter 3

Sex Rears Its Beautiful Head

AT the age of eight I gathered that the time was approaching when I should be leaving home for the greater part of the year and going to a private school. That, I was led to believe, was a place of pure delight where I should meet all sorts of new and exciting friends. My parents went off on various expeditions with a view to finding a suitable seminary which would advance my learning (if anything connected with me could be termed learning) and still leave them with a small income on which to exist.

I neither looked forward to nor dreaded the prospect of a boarding school. It was something that seemed to happen to everyone sooner or later, and if other small boys had survived the ordeal there seemed no good reason why it should prove beyond my capacities. Eventually I learned that Cothill House near Abingdon had been chosen for me. It was a small establishment and the fees were but £30 a term. Looking back at old school groups — of about thirty odd boys and some five or six assistant masters — I am at a loss to understand how anyone succeeded in making a living out of it. I reckon the junior masters cannot have earned much more than £150 a year. I suppose they made a little extra by tutoring backward boys in the holidays or perhaps they sought shelter in "digs" which they shared with some spinster sister who taught music in Richmond.

And so it was that on May 4th 1908 I joined a cluster of boys and masters at Paddington Station *en route* for Oxford. Two days later, when I was acquainting myself with my new surroundings, I received a letter from my mother who had obviously expected tearful scenes at the moment of departure. "We thought you were as brave as a lion," she wrote. Frankly this surprised me. Such a thing as any sort of emotional demonstration had never entered my head before.

I soon found out that the educational side of the school was on a somewhat higher mental plane than that to which I had become accustomed with my daily governess. My mind flitted back to my first lessons some four years previously. "Ann had an ox." In itself this was a harmless enough statement but when, to improve my handwriting, if you could have called my crude, unformed scratches writing, I was instructed to re-write this sentence no less than twenty times, I was not only sure of Ann's unlikely possession but as far as I was concerned she could have died a quiet and dignified death. On the other hand I give full marks to dear Miss Holmes (the name of my former governess) for her powers of imagination. "The sign of the Cross cut on to the forehead" was her answer to my query as to the exact meaning of the word "circumcision". This sounded reasonably credible and I took her at her word, nor do I blame her for her deception. After all, she was there to give a small boy elementary lessons, she had neither the qualifications nor ambition to turn her teaching into medical schooling.

Anyhow, here I was four years later grappling with the intricacies of Latin. In those days almost every Latin textbook started with the word "mensa" which we were told meant a table. I could never have believed that a simple article of furniture could be made so dreary or complicated. The intricacies and nuances of, what one would have thought was a fairly simple word, were beyond belief. To be asked to define it sent me into a paroxysm of nerves, all it seems to little purpose. The emphasis laid on it however gave the impression that the Romans thought of little else, whereas I suspect that if the truth were known tables to them had a certain rarity value.

Throughout my schooldays I found that it was the masters who were almost invariably kind to one and that it was usually at the hands of the other boys that one was made to suffer. I remember that in one of my first games of cricket

SEX REARS ITS BEAUTIFUL HEAD

I was placed in the outer field where a ball was extremely unlikely to come my way. The master in charge of the game drew the attention of the captain of the side to this fact. "Look," he said, "Nickalls is completely wasted out there." "Not much waste, sir," retorted the captain and then in case I hadn't heard, he repeated in the loudest possible voice, "Not much waste." How I longed to be able to emulate the worm at my feet and withdraw myself into the darkness and hoped-for oblivion of the kindly earth. Just how beastly can small boys be to one another; not much worse than small girls, I suspect.

My initial efforts at football were no more successful. I enjoyed cricket, but I loathed football. To hate such a splendid, manly game was the sign of a ne'er-do-well milksop. I remember on one particular occasion I was sent to keep goal. Cold and shivering, I was for some time enabled to watch the battle from afar without becoming involved. At last the moment arrived when to my horror it became obvious that I should have to take some part in the proceedings. I ran forward, grasped the ball, and threw it smartly between the goalposts I was meant to be defending. Sheer nerves; though to others it was quite obvious that I was not quite right in the head.

Every day there was an hour's break before lunch. We could do what we liked, which meant that we were meant to go out on to the football field and kick the ball around. There was no compulsion but it was the accepted thing to do. I, needless to say, didn't conform. I preferred to sit at my desk and work out rhymes and verses for my own amusement. Here was proof, if proof were needed, that I was not quite normal. My father arrived, quite unexpectedly, at the school one day. Having greeted him with the usual embraces, I enquired the reason for his surprise visit. It soon became obvious that he had been sent for by "Doggie", Dauglish, the Headmaster. "Doggie is a bit worried about you, old boy," he started. "Instead of going out and kicking a football about with the other boys, you seem to want to stay indoors and write poetry." Obviously there was something slightly queer about me. "Shouldn't I have more fun if I joined the others on the football field?" he enquired. For his sake I agreed to try. I kept my promise. I loathed it and my best efforts were rewarded with but little improvement or success.

The great social occasion of the summer term was the Fathers *v* Sons cricket match. It took place on Saturday, and on Sunday we were free to spend the day with our parents in whatever way they chose. The mid-morning arrival of our parents from Oxford in a two-horse brake was a moment of tremendous excitement. They seldom looked their best on arrival. The six-mile journey had been both leisurely and dusty. There was a boy called Hull whose people (other boys' parents were always termed "people") more affluent than the majority arrived in their own majestic Daimler. If memory serves me right their particular model was known as "The Silent Knight". All day long clusters of boys were allowed five minutes to go and gaze at this awe-inspiring monster. I can see them now looking it over in reverential wonder. Many were so overcome that they removed their caps in its presence.

In due course the match began. I had never seen my father play cricket before, and felt a certain pride in his performance when he hit boundaries off five successive balls. Doggie rushed out on to the pitch and whispered to him, "For God's sake get out, Guy, you'll be killing one of those boys in a minute." My father obeyed and placed an easy catch into the hands of mid-off on the last ball of the over. The Fathers' side was captained by Dickie Shaw. We were not on christian name terms, although he was by marriage a vague relation on my mother's side of the family. He had played cricket for Oxford in his day and some thirty-five years later became the first Bishop of Buckingham. I was low in the batting order of the school eleven and he put himself on to bowl against me. I can see his first delivery now. The ball broke in sharply from the off. I took a wild swipe at it and to my father's huge delight put it out of the ground. I must own that this particular fluke was the zenith of my cricketing career. Later that evening the Bishop, or the Archdeacon as he then was, had to catch a train. He was in no mood to miss the finish of the match so during the tea interval he changed back into his Archdeacon's clothing — gaiters, sash and all. Bowling in this rig was an unusual sight and reminded one somehow of a pirate ship running before the wind in full sail.

At Cothill, someone in the dim and distant past had had cement slides constructed. They were about sixty feet long, three feet wide, approximately three inches in depth. When frost seemed imminent they were flooded. At one end our momentum was brought to an abrupt halt by a mattress hung against the wall of the carpenter's shop. The return journey was made on a parallel slide which ended in our hopping off on to the frozen turf. I had never seen artificial slides before, or since, but they gave us a lot of fun. Mention of the carpenter's shop reminds me of Mr. Short who taught us carpentry — a large, jovial rumbustious figure with a short, red beard and blue eyes. He wore small, gold-rimmed spectacles which seemed almost entirely encased in the pink flesh which drooped from underneath his eyebrows and jutted upwards from his red fleshy cheekbones. I think in his home town, which was Abingdon, he must have been known as "something of a card". We were practising the high jump one day when Mr. Short arrived on the scene. The crossbar was set at about 3 ft. 6 ins., and Mr. Short made so bold as to say that he could clear it. As he weighed about eighteen stone, there were cries of, "Go on, Mr. Short. Go on." Whereupon Mr. Short approached the crossbar, knocked it on to the ground and with a naughty little wink skipped over it. This left no doubt that he was "a bit of a wag". On my first introduction to him he asked me what I would like to make. He reeled off a number of possibilities and ended by enquiring, "Or what about your own coffin." At this quip he slapped his thighs and bellowed with laughter. I took him seriously and began making rapid mental calculations as to my probable dimensions at the time of my demise. It didn't really matter what you wanted to make, your first term was occupied in constructing a bookcase which no one wanted. After that one could be promoted to rabbit or ferret hutches. I was rather keen on wooden trays, which did yeoman service in my home for many years to come.

At the prep school age boys are prone to a dreary list of contagious diseases—mumps, measles, chickenpox. Not one of them escaped us. Luckily there was a corrugated iron shanty down the road, known euphemistically as the Sanatorium. This contained a dormitory of six or seven beds and was presided over by a dear, God-fearing old couple—Mr. and Mrs. Stone. That they were good people I have no doubt. One evening I was describing a show I had seen in London during the previous holidays. I owned up to the fact that I had been particularly taken by the leading lady, "absolutely spiffing" was how I described her.

They did not approve of this giddy world beyond the Sanatorium. There was a momentary silence. Mrs. Stone spoke first, "An actress? Aw it's a wicked life." To this Mr. Stone assented mournfully. It was obvious to them that I was heading helter-skelter for eternal damnation. The subject of the stage was never mentioned again.

An extensive outbreak of measles engulfed us on one occasion. There were too many for the Sanatorium, so two dormitories in the school were given over to the victims. Sheets were hung over the door and the floors liberally besprinkled with "Sanitas", accompanied by all the other outward and visible signs of up-to-date hygiene. I was one of the first cases. I was quite ill, of that I was left in no doubt, especially when one of the oil lamps appeared to leave the mantelpiece, turn over, bounce on its glass shade and right itself without so much as a tinkle of broken glass. My sufferings were mitigated to a certain extent by the introduction of a trained nurse, for whom I conceived a grand passion. It was true that her coiffure was inclined to be a little untidy; my companions dubbed her golliwog, but that didn't count, nor was I able to conceal from them my abject adoration. They taunted me with this doggerel of their own composition:

> Oliver and Golliwog
> Walking in the misty fog

SEX REARS ITS BEAUTIFUL HEAD
Oliver kisses her
She says "I luv yer"

In a week or so I returned to the accustomed routine. The measles epidemic continued. I was surprised to find that on my return one of the assistant masters, who wasted a good deal of time trying to teach me mathematics, had turned into a roaring sadist. I must own that at that time I had never heard of the word. The whole classroom became a Dickensian nightmare. If some wretched boy was unable to answer a question the master in charge fumbled behind the blackboard and produced a cane which he brandished and swished about in such a threatening manner that our legs turned to water. Nor did it end with threats. Any incorrect answer from a boy was usually followed by his being summoned on to the platform, made to bend over "Tighter! Tighter!" and then with the tightness to his liking he administered three brutal blows on the bottom, followed by a request that you resume your seat. Back in his place the sobbing boy had to admit that these warm attentions had not enlightened his understanding. I know it happened to me. Such a statement, though perfectly true, was of no avail. The beatings continued. Dr. Squeers at the zenith of his brutality was unable to hold a cane to our tormentor. The extraordinary thing was that such was our loyalty, or was it our fear, that not one of us breathed a word of this orgy of flagellation to any other master. I suppose this astonishing state of affairs lasted only for two or three weeks. It seemed two or three years.

One day we were summoned into the big schoolroom, "Pie jaw from old Doggie" was the comment as word was passed from boy to boy. When we had taken our seats we were told that our flagellator had left and that we were not to ask what had happened to him as we should not be told. A week or so later we were summoned again and told that our tormentor had returned. He would not be teaching, though we would see him pottering about the garden. We were not to go and speak to him nor ask him where he had been. And there, as far as we were concerned, the matter ended. It was not for ten or fifteen years that I learned some sort of garbled explanation of the affair, and "affair" was the operative word. However untrue it may have been, I was informed that on the conclusion of the measles epidemic my darling "Golliwog" had returned to her normal duties with our master in hot pursuit. This gave me a certain latent pleasure. After all I'd spotted her first and she had aroused my puny lust as she had my teacher's. Whether unfulfilled lust (I am assuming it was unfulfilled) is liable to turn one into a ferocious monster I have no idea, but it seems to have done so in this case.

I repeat that none of what I have just recounted is necessarily true. All I know is that by Edwardian standards something slightly unsavoury must have occurred. The number of boys in the school fell to about twenty-six and poor old Doggie continued with his duties as a man half-stunned by this ghastly blow. In fact I am certain it contributed to his comparatively early death at the age of forty-nine some ten years later.

Never was there a more endearing, lovable man than "Doggie". He simply didn't deserve his cruel luck. For instance, it was customary for one of the assistant masters to perform on the organ at the local parish church, for which, during term-time, the school provided the choir. On his first Sunday there our organist surprised us all by belting out the opening and stirring chords of "Onward Christian Soldiers" just as we had embarked on our recitation of the Creed. It transpired that although he was by no means tone deaf he was certainly stone deaf. The whole of the next day he was occupied in packing his bags. I was sorry for him. Come, go, arrive, depart. His whole life it seems must have been reduced to a lifelike imitation of perpetual motion. For Doggie another piece of sheer bad luck. But why this handicap had not been discovered previously I fail to understand.

Like many other men Doggie had his foibles. Baden-Powell had just founded the Boy Scout movement. Doggie, for some reason, took a dim view of it. This was extremely awkward, as my father had thrown himself wholeheartedly

SEX REARS ITS BEAUTIFUL HEAD

into the work and became Scout Commissioner for South Bucks. My brother and myself were duly enrolled in the Eagle Patrol. On one occasion the most blood-curdling sounds were heard emanating from the lavatory, occupied by my father. My mother thought he was having a fit and rushed to his assistance. It was something of an anticlimax when she discovered that he was passing the time by practising the patrol's rallying signal—the cry of an eagle.

The highlight of one scouting year was the gathering of Scouts from all over the world. We were to go into camp in Windsor Great Park, and at a tremendous jamboree we were to be inspected by the King. My mother wrote to ask if we could be given special leave for one night in order to attend. Back came the reply: "Dear Mrs. Nickalls, I really must protest..." and so we missed the jamboree.

My father was very keen that I should learn boxing. The noble art played no part in the school curriculum. However, a brutal Irish sergeant who was hired to put us through the agonies of P.T. was put on to teach me boxing. We were allotted the squash court—a most unsuitable venue for our activities. Looking back, I don't think my instructor had any qualifications for teaching boxing. His method consisted of punching me into a corner of the court and then adjuring me to "Fight your way out, Nickalls. Fight your way out." It was never suggested that I should don shorts or zephyr for these lessons. I performed in my everyday shirt and my trousers or knickerbockers. There was no question of my taking a bath (there were no showers) after my strenuous efforts. Wringing wet with sweat, I would repair to the classroom, my clothes gradually drying out on me during the course of the day. As we were allowed only one hot bath and two cold baths every week, I must have stunk to high heaven.

When I first went to the school it was customary for some of the smaller boys to be given private tuition by the sallow-faced daughter of the local parson. I never got to know her very well, though I have no reason to think that she wasn't a thoroughly nice person. Unfortunately she suffered from the most virulent halitosis. Whenever opportunity offered, I turned my head away in horror. "Look at me when I'm speaking to you," she would command. Holding my breath I faced her again. When I could hold it no longer I turned my head quickly, took a deep gulp of fresh air, and faced her again. The whole performance was very distracting and I didn't learn very much.

It was my last term at Cothill and letters having passed between Doggie and my father it was arranged that Doggie should disclose to me the facts of life. So we had our little chat. Doggie was a bachelor and I have a feeling that his experience of the sexual act was, to say the least of it, extremely limited. There was gloomy talk of tubes and other carnal paraphernalia. In fact the whole business was made to sound like a laboratory experiment. Anyhow I never really liked science, or "stinks" as it was invariably called. His whole explanation sounded most distasteful, to such an extent that it might have turned me into a roaring misogynist for the rest of my days. I was also warned against the machinations of the older boys at my public school who would try to get into bed with me. I was a very ugly little boy and they never did.

In the summer term of 1912 I took my Common Entrance for Eton and passed into Lower Fourth (i.e. one form from the bottom). This designation is no longer in use. Standards have risen to such an extent that were I to submit these papers again today it is almost certain that I should "fail to satisfy the examiners".

The end of my last term was approaching. At Cothill there were all sorts of schoolboy rites connected with the last three Sundays of every term. The third from last Sunday was "button Sunday" when we all went to church with the bottom button of our waistcoats left undone. The second Sunday before our departure was known as "cock hat Sunday" which was marked by our going to church with our straw hats, which we wore for churchgoing both in winter and summer, perched at curious angles on our heads. The last Sunday was "Blub Sunday", when you were supposed to go round the school taking revenge, by reducing to tears, all those boys who had been beastly to you during the past

SEX REARS ITS BEAUTIFUL HEAD

term. "Cock hat Sunday" coincided with another chore. We had to enclose in our Sunday letter home a printed notice asking where our parents wished us to be deposited when the authorities had at last got rid of us. I can remember the wording to this day: "Those going to Paddington will catch the so and so train from Oxford. Those proceeding to Didcot, Swindon and the west. . . ."

On the final evening at "prayers" we sang the special end-of-term hymn:

> Lord, dismiss us with Thy blessing,
> . . . .
> Let Thy father-hand be shielding
> Those who here shall meet no more.

If it was one's last term one was supposed to allow a discreet, nostalgic tear to trickle down one's cheek during its singing. I accomplished this without too much difficulty. I loved acting. Somehow it all reminded me of those delightful verses of Harry Graham when he wrote of the conscientious parson who announced:

> . . . what proper hymns there be
> For those of riper years at sea.

The next morning, prior to our departure, there was much hearty hand-shaking accompanied by promises that one would write and keep in touch. Promises, I may say, that were but rarely fulfilled. Within the hour we had departed on our several ways to Paddington, or to Didcot, Swindon and the west.

Chapter 4

The Happiest Years of My Life?

It is with a certain shame that I have to admit that I did not greatly enjoy my time at Eton. That doesn't mean that during the five years I was there, amongst all the doubts and uncertainties that beset me, there were not some experiences which brought me great happiness. I would add also that had I been blessed with a son I would have sacrificed a great deal to send him there in the hope that he would have been able to make more of it than I did.

The truth was that, in modern parlance, I was "wringing wet". Ludicrously sensitive, terrified of what other boys might be thinking of me, over-anxious to do the right thing, and completely unable to stick up for myself. No such inhibitions beset my younger brother, who didn't give a damn what his contemporaries thought about him and, although small for his age, was perfectly capable of giving as good as he got and extremely popular with all and sundry. Those were the days when the top hat was part of our everyday dress. To some boys this was an irresistible target; to be knocked off the wearer's head, used as a football and eventually returned to the owner in a dilapidated condition. I never had the slightest desire to indulge in this particular form of high spirits. I never retaliated. It all seemed so childish. I don't think I was a prig but I was completely defenceless and, I repeat, wringing wet.

My parents were by no means well off. They made great financial sacrifices on behalf of my brother and myself and I always regret that I found myself unable to make the most of the opportunities my expensive education presumably gave me.

Those were the days when compulsory games were almost a religion in themselves. In the Michaelmas "half"

THE HAPPIEST YEARS OF MY LIFE?

(the Eton synonym for term) you were forced to play football four times a week and to record the fact that you had done so by putting a mark against your name on a list pinned to the House notice board. The form of football we played was called the Eton Field Game, which ensured that as many boys as possible were fully employed in an exhausting struggle for every minute of the hour-long game. If your play did not come up to the required standard you were, as likely as not, summoned that same evening by the Captain of Games of your particular House, given a short lecture on the value of the team spirit, commanded to put your head under a table and beaten "for slacking". It didn't end there. You earned the opprobrium of being a filthy little softy whilst great surprise was expressed that you didn't like such a splendid game.

There was one other boy I was fairly sure was experiencing the same sort of miseries as myself. His frame and features seemed ill-attuned to the Eton top hat and tail coat, and he seemed almost as defenceless as myself. His name was Sacheverell Sitwell. I don't think we ever spoke and I doubt whether he ever knew my name. We were on sympathetic, nodding terms when we passed each other in the High Street. He seemed to be singled out for ill usage. I can remember the exact spot where one little beast, spotting him in the distance, announced, "Hullo, here comes Sachy. Let's barge him off the pavement." This he proceeded to do. All so pointless!

At Eton I joined the craze for keeping white rats or rather one white rat. I found it companionable, friendly and very clean. During waking hours it would snuggle happily in my inside breast pocket. In the interests of hygiene I lined my pocket with a piece of blotting paper—a precaution I may say which never really seemed necessary. It never tried to leave my pocket. It was perfectly safe, therefore, to take it into the classroom with me and on one occasion, such was my confidence, I gave it a little run along the top of the pew in chapel. At this time my father was making bi-annual visits to America. On one occasion he arrived with a batch of bullfrogs which he kept in the hand basin of his cabin on the passage home. He was not popular with his fellow passengers, whose ears never became attuned to the croaking chorus which emanated from his cabin every evening. They were brought as a present for a contemporary of mine, one Donald Leney, whose spare time was spent adding considerably to the attractions of the Eton Museum by the introduction of various aquaria and other interesting exhibits. I remember that he had a young crocodile (or was it an alligator) which spent a somewhat boring existence in a hip bath. It hissed ferociously whenever anyone went near it. It was quite comfortable, its water being kept at a nice tropical heat by the flame of one solitary candle which burned continuously underneath its bath.

In addition to football, on one day in each week we were taken for a run. This meant a run of some three miles with a short break half way. This would have been an invigorating and welcome exercise had not the boy in charge assumed that every boy could run at the same pace. The mileage was covered as though it were a sprint race. Those who lagged behind the leaders were assumed to be idle and were goaded to further efforts by a hearty kick on the bottom or a swish on the back of the calves with a nice supple twig.

The Spring term brought relief from this type of torture. Then for recreation you had a chance of playing squash rackets, fives, or of following the beagles. I always nurtured a secret ambition to become Master of the Beagles, or at least one of the whippers-in. This ambition was never to be fulfilled, although I whipped-in and on a few occasions actually hunted beagles in the holidays. My hopes ran high on one occasion when the Master—Hugh Kindersley—handed me his whip and asked me to function in that capacity. Here I thought was my chance. It may have been, but as it turned out it came to nought. As a small boy, with what awe did I watch the immaculately polished hound van drawn by a pair of chestnuts make its appearance at midday outside Upper School. And with what envy did I watch the teenage Master accompanied by his Whips, all of them accoutred in velvet peaked caps and jackets with brass buttons, and accompanied by the kennel huntsman, mount

THE HAPPIEST YEARS OF MY LIFE?

the box and drive away to some distant meet. How glorious it all looked. The brass buttons I have referred to bore the insignia E. C. H. (Eton College Hunt). It is recorded that years before, when E. C. Hawtrey was Headmaster, he had asked to be allowed to inspect a button. Having done so he smiled approvingly, supposing E. C. H. to signify a charming compliment to his own popularity.

The summer school time gave me untold pleasure. Racing down to the Boat Houses, or Rafts as they were known, one jumped into a boat and sculled oneself up the river or got into a pair-oar and practised for some race or other, with a delicious cool bathe in prospect, as a reward for your exertions, either at Cuckoo Weir, Ward's Mead or Athens, according to your position in school. Cuckoo Weir and Ward's Mead were backwaters of the Thames, with green mown banks on either side. Athens was in the mainstream of the Thames. Those were the days when the river was so clear that one could see six or seven feet down into its watery depths. Since then the authorities have had to build an elaborate artificial pool. This was brought about by the waters of the Thames assuming a permanent weak coffee colour. At the time it was suspected that this polluted water might have been responsible for the various cases of polio amongst the boys. A few years back I was told by the then Headmaster, Robert Birley, that he had approached the health authorities with a view to ascertaining whether they had any statistics which would prove that there was a connection between pollution and polio. Their reply was in the negative. The Headmaster returned to the subject and asked them whether they could say with any certainty that there was no connection between the two. Again the answer was in the negative. In the circumstances, purely as a precautionary measure, the swimming pool was built. Undoubtedly it is a fine piece of work, though I cannot believe that for sheer unadulterated pleasure it can compare to our dear old natural haunts.

It was important, should you find yourself a lower boy in your second summer, that you should distinguish yourself, however slightly, either in the lower boy sculling or in the lower boy pulling (or pair-oar race). If you could manage this you were pretty sure to get your "boats" the following year. I won't go into the intricacies of being included in the "boats", except to say that if the school eight was your ultimate aim, as it was mine, then your inclusion in "boats" was, so to speak, the first rung of the ladder towards the attainment of that goal. In the circumstances I consulted my father, who advised me to have a look round at my colleagues and invite the biggest boy I could find to try his luck with me in the pulling (coxed pair-oar). I was lucky in a way. It wasn't very long before I espied an enormous Frenchman by the name of de Castéja — Comte de Castéja. I put forward a tentative invitation which to my great joy was accepted. I was as small for my age as he was big for his. He towered above me. He was not only tall but rotund, with pink cheeks whilst on his upper lip he sported an incipient dark moustache. I always understood that in later years he became a distinguished auction bridge player. He gave the impression of being mature beyond his years. He moved slowly, never got ruffled and spoke in slow rather deliberate tones without the trace of a French accent. We never had any sort of disagreement and for the next three or four years we remained on the friendliest terms. As soon as it got round that we had paired up for the "pulling" I was approached by various evil-tongued little boys and the conversation proceeded on these lines. "I say, Nickalls, you're not going in for the pulling with Castéja?" "Yes," I would reply, "why not?" "You know he's got two or three illegitimate children over in Paris." I turned a deaf ear to all such suggestions. It was obviously completely untrue, and after all what business was it of mine? We came in second, which made our promotion the following year a virtual certainty. I shall never forget how, as we were getting out of the boat after the race, my father came rushing up in a state of high excitement mingled with pride. He gave Castéja a congratulatory slap on the back and then to my utter horror exclaimed, "Well rowed, Count, old boy." Oh, how shaming! Why must he say that? By way of thanks, Castéja gave him a self-deprecatory, unemotional, world-weary smile.

THE HAPPIEST YEARS OF MY LIFE?

It may be argued that indulgence in games is all part, if not the most important part of a sound education. This is not a belief to which I would subscribe. In fact the over-emphasis of the importance of prowess on land or water was, I think, a great weakness in the education at Eton as it pertained in my day. Nowadays, I believe, they strike a far happier balance. Not so long ago I visited the new drawing schools on a half-holiday afternoon; there I found boys drawing and painting and practising their hand at lino cuts. How I should have loved to have had similar opportunities! But in my time, had anyone shown a preference for art as opposed to chasing a muddy football across a sodden field, all hell would have been let loose.

There were only two masters who were allowed to administer the birch or the cane—the Lower Master and the Headmaster. The Lower Master was responsible for meting out punishment to the "lower boys", whilst the Headmaster confined his beating energies to the so-called "uppers". There was, God knows why, a variation in the methods of administration. The Lower Master used the birch, the Headmaster a good stout cane. I have always understood that the parents of birched boys received a bill for 10/-, the cost of the birch which was listed under the pseudonym of "School Medicine". Never having experienced either, it is difficult to assess the relative "merits" of the weapons involved. The misdemeanours which called for corporal punishment from either of these awe-inspiring gentlemen were various. Slackness in school was one. The argument, I presume, being that what the masters had failed to teach you in the classroom, they could inject by means of physical force. Being caught out of one's house at night; a casual afternoon's visit to the Windsor Races or a late night supper over at Skindles in Maidenhead—would be certain to earn a beating or very possibly permanent expulsion from the school.

Birch or cane—the former would seem to be the more gruesome business. There was a birching block on which the culprit, having taken down his trousers, was requested to take up an appropriate position. Over and above that there was a college servant ready and willing, if necessary, to hold the victim at a suitable angle.

Sometimes one found that on entering a classroom a birching had just taken place. With an eager sadism, so prevalent in the young, one started collecting the branches and twigs of the birch. If one had the luck to find a twig bearing definite traces of blood it became something of a prized trophy. The Headmaster's execution was much on the same lines but not so exciting for the non-malefactors. No twigs! No blood!

Having recalled that only two masters could beat boys, it would be wrong to suppose that that was the end of corporal punishment. Our public school system has ordained that boys are divided into "Houses". These Houses are presided over by a Housemaster. You would be wrong in supposing that he was entitled to wield the cane. He was not; but for certain boys in his House there were no such restrictions. Each House has or had a caucus of seven or eight of its most prominent boys, whose use of the cane is or was almost a nightly entertainment. To lose a game of football by what was considered an unreasonably large margin called for the cane, as did being insufficiently willing to risk breaking a leg or a collarbone at football in pursuit of victory for the House. Obviously the Eton "Field Game" was invented to give pleasure to its participants. This, in my case, it signally failed to do. One of its least endearing aspects was when the uppers, released from their studies, strolled down to see how their lower boys were doing. Invading the field they would proceed to beat you on the bottom with their umbrellas as though to give a foretaste of what was to come, and it usually did, if you failed to go hard enough in the bully.

Before going to Eton my father had warned me against the "louts", as he termed them, who cheered on the side lines without partaking themselves. "If you're sufficiently keen on a game, partake in it," he used to say. "Don't sit back and cheer on the side lines."

It so happened that one year my House were in the semi-final of the House Cricket Cup. "M'Dame" or

THE HAPPIEST YEARS OF MY LIFE?

Matron, as she is usually termed in other schools, met me on the afternoon of the match and asked me if I was not going along to cheer for the House. Not realizing that I was committing a ghastly error I said that I was going to improve my sculling by going to Queens Eyot (where one could get tea) and back — a distance of some ten miles — a fair distance for a small boy in a heavy boat. Quite unaware that I had done anything wrong I was, that evening, summoned to the Library — the Caucus of prominent boys of the House to which I have already referred. The Captain of the Eleven, John Heathcoat Amory, having worked himself into a furious temper, then addressed me. "Why hadn't I been supporting the House at the match? D'you care a damn what the House does? Put your head under that table." And he administered eight cracking swipes which he managed to make curl round my thighs in a particularly agonizing way.

I had better admit that a year or so later I beat a boy for some misdemeanour on the river. The difference between myself and Amory was that whereas I had the gravest doubts about my own action, I don't suppose he gave his a second thought. Nor do I think that it occurred to him that, somewhere, somehow, the system was at fault. I only know that his punishment was so severe that I still bore traces of my originally bluish purple weals eighteen months later. So much for paternal advice!

I progressed steadily, if not brilliantly, up the school. I suppose like a great many other boys I studied my books just sufficiently to keep me out of serious trouble. And then with just one more year in front of me I faltered. For no apparent reason I failed to satisfy the examiners in at least two subjects. I rather dreaded my next meeting with R. S. de Havilland, my House Tutor. I need have had no qualms. I saw him in the offing. He came up and in the friendliest possible way remarked, "Well, not much luck." "I'm afraid not," I replied. "I think," he continued, "you'd better specialize in history." At that time I couldn't think why. The subject had never been mooted before. I was, however, only too willing to fall in with his wishes. It took me some time to realize what that most lovable of men had in mind. He was doing all he could to ensure that I shouldn't run the risk of superannuation before the following summer when my boat-propelling services would most certainly be needed to help his House to do as well as possible on the river. If this was his idea, then it certainly succeeded. I avoided superannuation and his House won the Aquatic Cup, which was an annual trophy awarded to the House with most successes on the river.

As I have said before, at an early age I had developed the desire to write verse; and I did so, however inadequately, for my own amusement, in my spare time. I had a certain rhyming facility plus an ear for metre and rhythm, and had I received any help or encouragement I believe I should have responded. I have often thought how grateful I should have been had I, at Eton, been initiated into the bare bones of various verse forms. Unfortunately no such opportunities came my way. Yet it is not true to suggest that verse was completely neglected. Whilst one might have been profitably employed improving one's verse and prose style in one's own language, one was forced to try to turn a piece of Latin prose into elegiacs. To compose elegiacs in a language of which one had little real knowledge was for me mental torture and a wicked waste of time.

During the First World War there was a shortage of masters and temporary replacements had to be found. Some were good, some not so good. I was fortunate in that C. R. L. Fletcher came to live with de Havilland. I knew him only as a name — an historian who had written a short history of Britain which was interspersed with verses by Rudyard Kipling. I count myself lucky in that I got to know him very well. I admired him not only as a fine lecturer on history but as a staunch friend and a very human and sympathetic personality. When I went up to Oxford I used to go to tea with him on Sunday afternoons at his house in Norham Road. One such afternoon his dog — let's assume his name was Toby — started emitting sharp little barks as dogs often do in dreams. Mrs. Fletcher asked him to what he attributed the cause of Toby's barking. "I know perfectly well,"

THE HAPPIEST YEARS OF MY LIFE?

replied her husband, "Toby is a great one for etiquette. He is attending a wedding, one of his doggy friends has arrived not having a wedding garment and Toby doesn't like it." For some reason this simple explanation gave me a lot of pleasure. The last time I saw Fletcher was one day by the riverside. I introduced him to my future wife. Perhaps he caught a suspicion of a hard little glint in her eyes, for he turned to her and said, "You will be kind to him, won't you?" He need have had no fears, but I have treasured it ever since as a kindly reminder of our mutual affection. Another arrival from Oxford at that time was F. F. Urquhart — better known as "Sligger" Urquhart. Of him we were told that his father had fought at the Battle of Navarino (which would suggest that he had achieved fatherhood at a rather advanced age) and that he enjoyed the unique distinction of having introduced Turkish Baths into England. In him I found a wise and kindly man. I would have liked to have got to know him a good deal better, but I always had the feeling that his intellectual prowess was rather too much for my somewhat humdrum mentality and I was terrified of boring him.

With so many masters on active service the influx of others to take their places must have been something of a matter of chance. There was one I have in mind who never gained the confidence or popularity he may have deserved. I'm in no position to make a judgment at first hand, for as it happened I was never "up" to him. But it came to be generally accepted that somehow or other he was heartily disliked. Boys have cruel ways of getting even with mentors of whom they do not approve. In the early days of the 1914 War, prior to the introduction of conscription, recruiting bands descended on various likely spots, and having played a few soul-stirring patriotic numbers, thereby collecting a crowd, they paused. This was the signal for a sergeant to mingle with the crowd and, having singled out a likely recruit, to suggest that he joined up. On the occasion of which I am thinking the band had been playing in one of the smaller school yards, and had gathered a sizeable collection of boys and passers-by who were gazing at them through the stout iron palings surrounding the yard. Just as the sergeant was going about his work the master in question happened to stroll by. In a matter of seconds various boys had drawn the attention of the recruiting sergeant to the solitary figure bestriding the yard, and had suggested to him that he was a good recruiting prospect. The sergeant without a moment's hesitation approached the master in question. The actual conversation was lost in the noise of a hundred or so boys shouting "Go on, sir, join up! Your King and Country need you, sir. We don't!" Just how vicious can a pack of boys become when they realize that the chance of any sort of reprisal for their conduct is extremely remote.

The end of term examinations were known as "Trials". This means that some thirty or forty boys are shepherded into a classroom, the papers we were invited to answer were handed out and we were allowed some three hours to complete them under the vigilant eye of some master or other. On one occasion I found the master I have referred to above in charge of these proceedings. One clever little boy had completed his papers in little over an hour. Whereupon he took them up and deposited them on the desk of the master in charge and asked if he could go. "No, you can't," came the reply. "Resume your seat." Gladwyn Jebb, for that was his name, did as he was told. In a moment or two a certain *ennui* overtook him, so to pass the time he produced a watch from his waistcoat pocket and proceeded to wind it up. The noise produced by this ancient time-piece, reverberated round the room, and disturbed the master who gazed at Jebb with some distaste. His colour rose and glowering at the culprit he exclaimed, "I suppose you can't make much more noise with that watch, can you, young man?" Completely unperturbed, Jebb continued to wind the watch and replied, "I don't know, sir, I'll try." It seldom pays to be sarcastic with boys.

Some fifty years later I was repeating this episode to Robert Birley, who had just retired from his Headmastership of Eton. Referring to the master in question he asked, as though fearful of being overheard, "but you know what

THE HAPPIEST YEARS OF MY LIFE?

happened to him?" I had to admit that I knew nothing of his subsequent career. "You don't know what happened to him?" I couldn't begin to guess. I hardly thought he had done time. Having gazed furtively over his shoulder as though to make certain he was not being overheard, Birley replied in an awe-inspiring whisper, "he became Secretary of a Golf Club."

In meting out punishment it is curious how some masters succeed in arousing hatred and ill-will in their pupils while others can be just as severe and still retain their affection. A master at my private school would, for some misdemeanour or other, cause boys to turn the palms of their hands upwards and strike their desk with some force with the backs of their hands. This was a painful process. Sometimes he would vary the procedure and command some culprit, "D'you mind slapping yourself rather hard on the side of your face?" The boy gave himself a tap on his cheek, emitting a cry of "Oh, sir!" to suggest that he had hurt himself a good deal. He deceived no one. "Not hard enough. Do it as though you really mean it." The boy repeated the performance to the accompaniment of the inevitable "Oh, sir!" It was obvious that this time he really had hurt himself. "Thank you," said the master. "I never punish boys. I always make them punish themselves." I suppose that nowadays this would be looked upon as a brutal practice, yet we bore him no ill-will.

My time at Eton was drawing to a close. There were discussions with my parents as to my army career, which loomed ahead. I expressed a hope that I might join the Rifle Brigade. My mother made a strong plea for the artillery, as being safer than the infantry. I argued that owing to the extensive casualties in the infantry it was up to me to serve that branch of the service most in need of men. My father agreed with my point of view and that settled the matter. Beside the instruction afforded by the College O. T. C., it was felt that more experience would be no bad thing, and it was for this reason that on various occasions some of the older boys were set up to drill on the square with a battalion of the Coldstream Guards. This did me a lot of good. It wasn't comfortable. It wasn't meant to be. The square since those days has undergone a change. Nowadays, I believe, it boasts a tarmac surface, at that time it was dusty gravel. As we marched up and down, clouds of ochre-coloured dust collected on our sweaty faces which within a few minutes took on a matt-like surface which must have given the impression that we were about to face the film cameras. It was not long before I began to understand the meaning of real discipline. "Form fours," shouted the sergeant major. Then "as you were". This was repeated no less than four times. There was an ominous pause. "Put Corporal Hawkins under arrest" came the order. Thunderstruck, we stood at attention whilst Hawkins under close guard was marched off the parade ground. What ghastly things would happen to him we could only guess. As the sound of their footsteps died away and we waited for the clanking of chains, which seemed imminent, the sergeant major addressed us again. "I've formed fours four times for that man, and he hasn't moved once. One man has already lost his name this morning so we'd better buck ourselves up a bit." This was discipline with a capital "D" and it shook me considerably — which was just what it was meant to do.

In spite of these interruptions my last half was a particularly happy one. Besides victories in other races I got into the school "Eight", and there being no Henley Regatta at which to compete, a private match over the Henley course was rowed against Shrewsbury. In spite of some bad rowing on my part we were victorious.

I thought I would return to Eton for another half and continue there until I was called up. This would have been my sixth Michaelmas term time. I found I was to be instructed by Aldous Huxley in a certain classroom with which I was unacquainted. Several of us were in the same predicament. After unsuccessful attempts we found the room where he was presiding. As we entered, some ten minutes late, there were shouts from some of our colleagues who were already seated. "For God's sake don't come in, we've answered your names." This was Huxley's first day as a master and obviously he wouldn't know a single boy by

THE HAPPIEST YEARS OF MY LIFE?

sight, even if his extremely poor sight would have allowed it. Not wishing to let down our friends who had done their best for us, we beat a hasty retreat and returned to our respective Houses. We were spotted and a notice came round the next day. "Several boys shirked Mr. Huxley's school yesterday. Some of them were recognized but we expect the rest to own up." They failed to mention the names of those who had been recognized. "Thereby," as one of our number sarcastically remarked, "teaching us the true principles of British sportsmanship."

We were called before the Headmaster quite confident that he would understand our reluctance to betray our friends who had been so misguidedly kind to us. We told our story thinking we should receive some light reprimand. "That's all very well," replied Cyril Alington, "but I don't think you're all such early Christian martyrs as you make out." He scribbled on various pieces of paper, handed them to us and we left the presence. Once outside, eager to learn our fate, we scanned the pieces of paper; six hundred Greek "lines" with accents and breathings. A very savage sentence.

The next day I received my call up, and the following day I was receiving my Leaving Book from Alington. My "lines" I had not even begun. As I took leave of him I almost believed I had enjoyed every moment of my time at Eton; which was very far from being the truth.

Chapter 5

Pierrots In Uniform

It was in September 1917 that I was ordered to report to an Officers' Cadet Battalion. The company to which I was accredited was quartered in St. John's College, Oxford. The manpower situation was crucial. Three months' training was considered sufficient time in which to equip one to become an officer, providing that one was successful in the passing-out examination.

Our days were passed in drilling, physical training and bayonet fighting, interspersed with lectures on map and compass reading and other subjects considered necessary. Having gone through it all before, I became thoroughly bored. Unfortunately I showed it and received a warning that unless I bucked myself up a bit I shouldn't be allowed even to sit for the examination. However, no dire consequences ensued and at the end of my time I was duly commissioned.

At St. John's we formed a pierrot troupe and found ourselves much in demand. Our company commander was one of our number. He would oblige with a spirited rendering of "Phil the Fleuthers Ball". Another member rather fancied his particular interpretation of "I'm learning a Song for Christmas, to sing it on Christmas Night" which terminated with the couplet:

> But I shall look a mug (pronounced "moog")
> With my little brown jug (pronounced "joog")
> When I sing it on Christmas night.

One of our better singers assumed he was bringing emotional lumps into our throats with "That dear little old-fashioned town". My own contribution consisted of numbers from revues and musicals then running in London. I did a poorish imitation of George Robey ("The Prime Minister of Mirth"). Part of one of his numbers ran thus:

> She's a lady of unlimited allurements;
> A proclivity for passion she displays.
> A desire for osculation she evinces
> She's amorous and yielding in her ways.
> She's partial to promiscuous caresses;
> To the blandishments of Cupid she succumbs.
> She responds to demonstrations of affection;
> In other words she's thumbs!

At the beginning of the war a young man by the name of Basil Hallam, who had started in show business with a walking-on part in a musical, *The Passing Show*, worked his way up and sprung into prominence with a hit number:

> I'm Gilbert the Filbert
> The knut with a K
> The pride of Piccadilly
> The blasé roué.
> Oh Hades, the ladies
> Who leave their wooden huts
> For Gilbert the Filbert, the Colonel of the knuts!

For the benefit of those whose memories do not go back sufficiently far, it should be explained that a knut in those days was the modern slang for a fop or dandy, and that the reference to "wooden huts" was borrowed from a song of a still earlier era: "I wouldn't leave my little wooden hut for you".

"Gilbert the Filbert" swept the country, and Basil Hallam into the matinee idol class. He came down one afternoon to Eton and that was the only time I heard his rendering of the song in person. At that performance he sang another number which I had never heard before and have never heard since. It was a rather dashing song for those days and I have often wondered if the Eton authorities had bargained for anything quite so risqué. Part of the refrain ran:

A RAINBOW IN THE SKY

> Dear old Vicar
> It would make his heart beat quicker
> If he knew what Enid his eldest daughter did.

For it seems that this ultra-modern young lady would

> Come out stripped for Rugger
> Just to let the forwards hug her

and that

> Some of her phrases
> Would fairly force the daisies.

Poor Basil Hallam joined up. On the Western Front his observation balloon was struck. He jumped. Alas, his parachute failed to open.

I apologise for this long digression, but it will be understood that lyric writers everywhere were all trying to find a worthy follow-up to "Gilbert the Filbert" and that is how in my pierrot troupe's repertoire I found myself singing a really terrible song:

> I'm Reckless Reggie of the Regent Palace
> And I flirt with every gal
> First I flirt with Flora, then I flirt with Alice,
> I'm a real live Regent pal.
> I'm a rip, I'm a roarer
> When I flirt with Dora
> And the time that I have's not bad.
> I'm a knut, what what
> At the na-pooh trot
> Haw! Haw! I some bad lad.

I was told that my version of this song was first-rate. Looking back I am enveloped in shame. How I had the sheer nerve and audacity to tackle such nonsense I can't imagine.

The ordinary soldier directed much of his caustic wit to those who were "on the staff". There was a feeling that they were, on the whole, a lazy bunch who had somehow or other landed their staff jobs by pulling the correct strings. This, of course, in most cases was entirely unfair. Most of the jibes they endured for having landed themselves with what was known as "a nice cushy job" were prompted by malicious envy. Draping a piece of red flannelette round my peaked cap I would echo the general attitude with:

> I'm on the staff, I'm on the staff
> And upon my word I really had to laugh
> I'll perhaps look in the office say from half past two to three
> And the four and twenty lady clerks, they'll all attend to me.
> And the nicest of the lot will put the sugar in my tea.
> I'm on the staff, I'm on the staff.

At the end of December 1917 I took the necessary exam, passed and was commissioned to the Rifle Brigade, which I joined at Minster on the Isle of Sheppey early in the New Year. Here, I imagined, I should be engaged on normal battalion duties. I couldn't have been more wrong. The War Office had turned Minster into a depot for officers, and it was from there they were sent overseas to join the various units to which they were appointed. I think there must have been over a hundred officers on the strength and about the same number of other ranks. On arrival there, we were given a short lecture by the adjutant on the general curriculum to be followed. I was surprised to learn that our colonel, Patrick Talbot, did not expect us to undertake any military duties in the afternoon so long as we played rugger; so play rugger we did. I couldn't help feeling that it was a rather casual approach to the act of warfare. In France, the Germans launched their last desperate offensive in March and succeeded in breaking our lines—yet we continued to play rugger.

I cannot really remember what else we did there. Occasionally we were turned out to drill a platoon. Only a handful of picked officers were put on regimental duties. In fact it was not until I arrived on the Salonika front in June, that I was given my first experience of commanding a platoon.

Minster at that time presented a somewhat bizarre appearance. Before the war there had been an attempt to turn it into a seaside resort. I suppose they had intended originally to build some two hundred and fifty houses on a flat piece of land running down to the cliffs. Actually they had completed some thirty houses when the war had postponed all further constructional work. Streets had been laid out and kerb stones indicated the intended demarcation of roadways and pavements. By the time of which I am writing grass had overgrown all traces of these essentials; the impression it gave was of a number of houses scattered haphazardly over a green landscape. The houses were unoccupied and presented a somewhat dreary ghost-town appearance. On my arrival, a Nissen hut shared with some forty others was my sleeping quarters. Nothing wrong with that, except that one's sleep was constantly disturbed by drunks coming home at all hours of the night. There were not many outlets for amusement and I suppose that fact contributed to an excessive alcoholic intake. Some officers sought relief from the general boredom by visiting the Sheerness Hippodrome. One night I heard two of them, both a bit the worse for wear, discussing in blurred voices the merits of a certain lady of the chorus. "I say, old boy, I rather liked the look of that girl with the reddish hair." "Did you, old chap?" "You know the one I mean, the one fourth from the right." "Frankly I couldn't count them, but do you mean the one with the dirty knees?" "That's the one, the one with the dirty knees. Damned attractive!" "Goo night old boy." "Goo night, wish I hadn't had that last whisky." "Same here" and within a minute they were both snoring loudly.

I was fortunate enough to be transferred to one of the empty houses, which I shared with two or three others. It was a good deal more comfortable and civilized than my former surroundings. Our Mess and H.Q. were in the Minster Workhouse and the surrounding buildings. Once a week the band played during dinner. Patrick Talbot loved his band and it attained a very high standard considering that its members were constantly being drafted abroad and replaced by substitutes.

Another C.O. of my acquaintance had an absolute passion for his band. On one occasion a brass hat was dining with him on Mess Night. "I suppose it's jolly hard to keep this band of yours together — always being drafted overseas and that sort of thing?" "You're quite right it is," replied the C.O. "No sooner have they got into their stride than off they go. Perfectly sickening." Now in fact this colonel's passion for this band was carried to such lengths that in order to keep them together he refrained from drafting them overseas at all. About a year later the same brass hat paid another visit to the battalion on a Mess Night. By a piece of extraordinarily bad luck he had an astonishing memory for faces. He glanced at the band and there to his astonishment he recognized the violinist fiddling merrily away in the corner as being the same musician he had seen there the previous year. No words were exchanged on the subject but in a few weeks' time the C.O. was presented with a bowler hat.

One evening I received a note from the adjutant ordering me to report to a certain villa close to our H.Q. and to take along my kit for the night. I went along at the appointed hour and rang the bell, which was answered by a shout to enter and come upstairs. There I found two of my colleagues playing patience. "What am I supposed to be doing?" I asked innocently. "Oh," said one of them, "You've got to look after old so and so here and see he doesn't smoke too many cigarettes." I then realized what it was all about. "Old so and so" was under close arrest and it had fallen to my lot to guard him for twenty-four hours. They passed off uneventfully, though I can't help feeling that it was a bit casual on the part of the adjutant to omit to give a boy of eighteen (my age at the time) any hint of the duty to which he was being allotted.

As was customary in most units the battalion boasted its Amateur Dramatic Society. I remember that for one week they played *David Garrick*. I was much struck with the performance of the man who played the name part. In his silks and satins, his knee breeches, silver shoe buckles and lace cuffs, he displayed a complete grasp of the role. His movements were grace personified. His manipulation of his snuff box and spy glass, punctuated at intervals by a low bow with the left hand placed in the small of the back and the right hand performing a graceful sweep with his handkerchief held between the first and second fingers, was astonishing. Outside London I had never seen such a finished performance. The next day I was walking off the parade ground with a friend. "Here comes our David Garrick," he remarked. I couldn't believe my eyes for there coming towards us was a flat-footed, scruffy-looking little private carrying a latrine bucket in either hand. We stopped, he put down the buckets and then we congratulated him on his performance of the previous evening. It seemed impossible that this inconspicuous little man was the same god-like creature whom the night before had strutted the boards with such aplomb. We continued on our way. Looking over my shoulder I noted that "David Garrick" had picked up his buckets and resumed his sanitary duties. I never saw him again.

A few days later I was having tea in the Mess when a small piece of paper was placed in front of me. Its instructions were that I should join a troop train at Waterloo in three days' time and proceed overseas. A hardened old warrior opposite me knew what that slip of paper meant. He leant across and said, "I know exactly how it feels, old boy! You get a momentary spasm here", and he prodded that part of his anatomy where the first signs of a duodenal ulcer make themselves felt. He was quite right.

I noted that I had been drafted to the 4th Battalion of the Rifle Brigade, and was to proceed to Salonika. The 4th was one of the regular Battalions who had been sent to Salonika direct from India. I was delighted to learn that Rowley Marriott, one of my closer friends and exactly my age, was coming with me. We packed our kit and arrived at my parents' home at Farnham Royal somewhere around midnight. First thing next morning he was off to his own home near Rugby. I spent two glorious afternoons at Eton. There were some pair-oar races in progress and I sat lazily on the river bank. How wonderful it looked compared to the soul-destroying scenery of the Isle of Sheppey. The next day my father and young brother came to see me off. My father said goodbye and wished me good luck. He closed the door of the compartment, not realizing that three fingers of my left hand were resting in the hinge. They were squeezed flat. Agony! The train moved off. Some three weeks later I shed three blackened and dead fingernails in Greece.

Chapter 6

Hunting In No-Man's-Land

WE sailed from Southampton at dusk, noting the outline of Netley Hospital as we ploughed out into the Channel. It was not a comfortable night; too hot down in the saloon and too cold on deck. Our crew kept a sharp look-out for submarines. There were one or two false alarms. However, early the next morning we docked at Cherbourg without mishap. A railway ran alongside the quay and a variety of trucks were being shunted to and fro. We wondered whether we were to make the journey in one of those prison-like trucks marked "Hommes 40 Cheveaux 20". It was with some relief that we found we were to travel in ordinary passenger carriages, four of us in each carriage. Our destination was Taranto. We spent one night at a rest camp near Lyons, and another at Faenza in north Italy. There seemed to be no particular schedule governing our progress. Eventually we arrived at Taranto some ten days later.

After our night near Lyons we headed north and the scenery was much more interesting. It was warm and sunny and we climbed along the footplates until we arrived at one of those iron ladders, then an integral piece of equipment on all French trains. We climbed up on to the roof of the carriage and sat there hour after hour enjoying our surroundings. No one suggested that we should do otherwise. We were warned not to stand up on top of the carriage without making sure that we were not approaching a tunnel. On a previous trip one unfortunate man had done just this — with fatal results.

The train jogged along, rarely exceeding thirty miles an hour. By jumping from carriage top to carriage top one could cover the whole length of the train with little risk. I remember particularly the beauty of the whole setting as we approached Chambery. Meals were taken at some railside station and by dint of piling our luggage seat-high into the well of the carriage we were able to enjoy comparatively comfortable nights. On occasions the train would remain stationary for hours on end. If it happened to be at a small town or village we were told our time of departure and allowed to go out and find any amusement that might take our fancy. Usually, as soon as we walked out of the station we were immediately surrounded by a horde of urchins pimping for their so-called sisters. "You like jig-a-jig, mister? My sister, she very good. I take you to her. Bugger off!" These miniature procurers had on so many occasions failed in their objective that they added the two final words almost as though they were saving us the necessity to reply. Somehow, I found it strangely touching.

Our one night stay at Faenza enabled us to buy some of the local pottery. We sent this straight home and I was really rather surprised when I found it waiting for me, quite intact, some nine months later. The journey down the east coast of Italy was the least interesting part, except that the railroad skirted the seashore at intervals *en route* for Taranto. The train showed no sense of urgency on its progress south. Sometimes we would stop for a bare five minutes, at others for half an hour or more. On one such occasion only some fifty yards separated us from the sea. It was a gloriously sunny day. Three or four of the party felt that this was a heaven-sent opportunity for a bathe. They donned their bathing trunks, crossed the line and entered the sea. They were some twenty yards out from the shore when the engine gave a peremptory whistle preparatory to getting under way again. It now became a question as to whether the swimmers could regain the train before it moved off. It was a hilarious sight to watch them striking out for the shore, sprinting up the beach and in bare feet re-crossing the line at break-neck speed, urged on by roars of applause from their comrades in the train. The train was already moving as they flung themselves into the nearest carriage. They were in agony. The rough stones supporting the railway track sleepers had played havoc with the soles of their feet.

On another occasion the train stopped hard by an inviting-looking *ristorante*. This was too great a temptation. Two of the party thought that a drink would come as a welcome restorative. Having downed several Camparis and soda, they strolled out to rejoin the train. Much to their surprise and dismay they found it had moved off without them. Being men of resource they summoned the local taxi and went in pursuit. The snail-like pace of the train will be appreciated when I reveal that within half an hour they had overtaken it, signalled to it to stop and remounted. I never quite understood why the train travelled so slowly. It may be that the track was in bad repair or that it was difficult to raise any pressure of steam when the train was fired (as ours was) by logs of wood as opposed to the customary coal.

After what seemed an eternity, we arrived at Taranto and embarked on a boat to cross the Adriatic to Greece. By that time we had been joined by a party of about a dozen padres of various denominations. This posse of clergy, with their dog collars and the black, rank-denoting pips on their shoulder straps, caused an American on board to comment; "Say, by the number of you dominoes on board, you English must be a durn lot of rotters!"

Eventually we weighed anchor in the Gulf of Itea. It was dusk when we landed on the northern shore, and after dinner we went for a bathe. The warm Mediterranean water, heavily charged with phosphorous, gave a display of silvery miniature fireworks as we splashed about, and proved the most pleasing experience I had enjoyed on the whole journey. We were next told that a convoy of lorries would take us on a thirty-mile mountainous journey to where, once more, we would entrain. We would be leaving early the following afternoon. Reference to a map showed that we were quite close to Delphi, which lay some five miles up in the hills above us. I learned that some of the padres were planning a visit. I asked if I might join them. In order to fit in with our schedule and to avoid the full heat of the sun we planned to set out at 5.30 a.m. on the following morning.

The earlier stages of our journey, through copious olive groves, was pleasant enough and the hard, red-ochre coloured ground made walking easy. Then the way led up steep hills and we had to make several detours when we found ourselves encroaching on private property or when some snarling vicious-looking dogs indicated that our presence was very far from welcome. Eventually Delphi in all its glory, backed by the heights of Mount Parnassus, opened up before us. Its beauty was breath-taking. We were put in the charge of (for some unexplained reason) a French guide, who conducted us through the more outstanding ruins : the theatre with its wonderful acoustic properties, the stadium where the athletes as often as not ran up and down the arena swinging themselves around wooden poles placed at either end. The holes in the ground into which those poles were placed are visible to this day. We saw the remains of the Temple of Apollo. I recalled through my meagre classical knowledge that when pilgrims consulted the oracle there, the answers could be taken in several different ways. What, for instance, was the exact meaning of the answer which advised "Stand fast behind your wooden walls". I could only conclude that the whole mumbo-jumbo attributed to Apollo was a gigantic and money-making tourist attraction. In one of his books Osbert Lancaster records that poor old Aesop, of fable fame, was flung to his death from the heights of Mount Parnassus. "No doubt," he writes, "he had delivered some well-deserved wisecracks at the expense of the local administration." Finally our guide led us down to the baths. There to my utter horror, having cleared away some minor rubble, he ripped up slabs of the original mosaic paving, broke them into pieces and distributed them amongst us with the words, "No tell Museum, no tell Museum."

Eventually he conducted us to the modern museum ; in those days nothing much more than a large tin shanty. There stood a life-size statue of a glorious specimen of early manhood. As soon as one of the padres enquired naively as to his identity somehow I knew he would have done well to be less inquisitive. "Oh yes," explained our guide. "One of ze old emperors — he marry *le garçon* — this is he." Some of the ecclesiastical fraternity looked down their noses, others gazed ruminatively at the ceiling while others stubbed the ferrules of their walking sticks on to the stone flooring. There was an awkward silence. Quite obviously even such an oblique reference to homosexuality was a forbidden subject. After a cup of Turkish coffee at a nearby inn we were lucky enough to get a lift in a car that was returning to our camp.

I did not see Delphi again for forty-one years. On my next visit I was sitting in a bus and on the way there explained to two old ladies that I had not been there for nearly half a century. "Well," they asked as we arrived, "what do you think of it now?" I admitted that I could only reply in the words of Winston Churchill on being asked what he thought of the Niagara Falls on seeing them for the second time: "The principle's the same."

On my second visit, so carried away was I by the sheer beauty of my surroundings that I scribbled some random verses which I was foolish enough to show to one of my companions. "I suppose they're all right," he commented, "but they're fourth form stuff, aren't they?" He was probably right. It was some consolation however to be able to report to him a month or so later that, fourth form stuff or not, I had succeeded in getting them published.

One of the many pamphlets issued by the Greek Tourist Association suggests that the name Delphi is derived from the word dolphin and is appropriate owing to the number of dolphins which can be seen cruising around in the Gulf of Itea below Delphi. This in fact is what I wrote:

DELPHI

Disporting midst the olive groves
That cradle Delphi by the sea,
The shades of land-locked dolphins play
In purple-shadowed ecstasy.

HUNTING IN NO-MAN'S-LAND

When to these shores the ancients came
And made their way as men do still,
Through blue-grey clouds of olive trees,
To shrines and temples on the hill,

The gallant dolphins thought that they
Would follow where the ancients trod
And shape them in some friendly pool
A votive offering to their god.

But when to climb those sun-scorched slopes
Those valiant dolphins vainly tried
Returning to the olives' shade,
They one by one laid down and died.

Not theirs to seek Apollo's aid
Nor wear the victors' crown of fame
To Delphi, dolphins gave their all
To Delphi, dolphins gave their name.

And in those olive groves today
The shades of dolphins frisk and play.

On that first visit to Delphi, we lunched and packed ourselves into a convoy of lorries that took us on a hazardous, hair-raising journey through the mountains, to a railhead situated I suppose some forty miles north of Athens. Here we entrained once more on the final stage of our journey through Larissa to Salonika. It was during this journey that I saw storks in the wild for the first time. They had built themselves rooftop nests and, as they lowered their long legs preparatory to alighting on the tiles, I was surprised to see how clumsy they looked and how ill-equipped they appeared to be for that particular manœuvre.

By the time we arrived at Salonika we had been between two and three weeks on the journey. One would have thought there existed a less arduous route to our destination. We had, however, arrived safely, only running the risk of U-boat interference for a total of not more than thirty-six hours on the whole journey. At the base camp just outside the town we were to learn, for the first time, the stifling and claustrophobic experience of sleeping under a mosquito net at the height of the Macedonian summer. After a stay of two or three days we joined our battalion in the Struma Valley.

The adjutant introduced us to the colonel and we were drafted to our respective companies. Considerately they asked if two of us would like to stick together. Rowley Marriott and myself elected to take advantage of this offer and were taken along to our company commander, a comparative veteran of twenty-one who had fallen victim to recurrent attacks of malaria. He gave us a cordial welcome and we liked him straight away.

Our general surroundings were a matter of great surprise to us. We had expected trench warfare. It was conspicuous by its absence. The Struma Valley was a waste of swamp and marsh land flanking the Struma River. To say we were facing the Bulgars would give the wrong impression. We were facing them but at a distance, so I was informed, of some fifteen miles. In fact during the three or four weeks I was on that particular front I never so much as saw a Bulgar. Their positions were on some distant hills, ours hard by the river itself. They had a fairly good view of us. When scratch cricket matches were arranged, they never interfered; though once or twice when we held a battalion parade in full view of them, they, as much as to say "Big Brother is watching you" lobbed a few shells in our direction.

On the Salonika front there were far fewer casualties from shrapnel, rifle and machine-gun fire than there were in France. On the other hand, the ravages of dysentery and malaria kept our hospitals full to overflowing. There was one type of malaria euphemistically known as "benign". It recurred regularly. Plenty of the men took this as a matter of course and didn't even bother to report sick. On my first evening with the battalion I heard Huyse-Eliot, my company commander, remark quite casually to one of his lieutenants, "I've got a go of malaria. I'm going to lie down now. Come and see me about five. I shall probably be unconscious. If I am, don't do anything, but come back at nine

HUNTING IN NO-MAN'S-LAND

and if I'm still unconscious you had better send for the M.O."

Such military duties as we undertook were confined either to the early morning or late afternoon. From mid-day onwards the heat was unbearable, and every day after lunch we lay on top of our sleeping bags and underneath our mosquito nets, where we sweltered until the cool of the evening brought some relief. One morning I was sent out with a handful of men to sort out a heap of equipment which had been dumped completely haphazardly. It was an awe-inspiring, tangled mass some twenty-five feet high, covering an area about eighty by forty feet. It consisted of tyres, cookers, bundles of bivouacs, cases of bombs and every sort of military accessory one could imagine. We marked out sites near at hand so that the tyres were stacked in one area, the packing cases in another and so on. We had just started on this gigantic task when a brisk-looking staff officer approached me. He asked me if I understood what we were meant to be doing. Indicating the towering mass in front of us I replied that we were making a start on sorting it out. "You're quite right," he said. "You're here to bring order out of chaos." He seemed to be rather pleased with his own eloquence for he repeated "order out of chaos is the watchword of the day". I refrained from asking him what the hell he *thought* we were doing. It was my first encounter with a staff officer, and not a very inspiring one, yet my belief in the wisdom and efficiency of the majority of their kind remained unshaken.

No-man's-land abounded in game. Officers used to go out shooting in an endeavour to see what they could get to relieve the monotony of ordinary rations. Sometimes on these forays they would meet enemy officers — Bulgars bent on the same business. Amongst sportsmen there was no thought of mortal combat — one party would hold up their game to show the extent of their bag whilst the enemy would return the courtesy and each party would pass quietly on their way. My C.O., Colonel Railston, thought he could relieve the general monotony by forming a pack of hounds. He imported two couple of foxhounds which, when interbred with the local sheep dog, soon formed a sizeable pack. To avoid the heat of the day, and mounted on whatever steeds were available, we sallied forth and chopped four or five hares and two or three foxes before breakfast. Whenever we changed our quarters the assistant adjutant was sent ahead to find a suitable dugout for the pack. Two wretched privates were detailed to act as kennel huntsmen. They exercised the hounds every evening. By dint of continually cracking their whips they kept the pack in some sort of formation. At the same time they were wise enough to keep their proper distance. Quite obviously the men were terrified of this pack of wild-looking mongrels.

Rumours, which proved to be well-founded, began to filter through. One day a party of brass hats picked me up and gave me a lift in their car. They informed me, rather sadistically I felt, that we were soon to be moved to the Vardar front, where we should see some "real fighting". It seemed that the Greeks were to relieve us on the Struma and and we in our turn were destined to relieve the French on the Vardar.

Eventually a Greek officer arrived and was attached to our Company H.Q. I can remember his name to this day, Jean Nannos. It appeared that he was a bank manager from Athens. Having regard to the numerous Balkan wars that had been in progress during the past decade, I cannot help feeling that he had not had very much time to pursue his chosen profession. He carried a sword with him wherever he went. It was encased in a brass scabbard which had a fair-sized dent in it about half way up. This must surely have made the drawing and sheathing of the sword a somewhat strenuous process. It is perhaps unnecessary to mention that in the British Army the sword as an offensive weapon had long since been discarded and relegated to the role of a ceremonial gimmick. We asked him, therefore, why he carried a sword? It was essential he explained. "When we charge ze enemy, the officer draws his sword." Suiting his action to the words he held it aloft and brandished it with threatening gestures. "My men zey see ze sword and follow it." We watched in stupefaction this

A 'kill' in No-Man's Land. Hunting in Struma Valley, Macedonia, July 1918

G. O. Nickalls bow and steers with R. S. C. Lucas. Winners of Silver Goblets 1920 and 1922

Our wedding, November 5, 1929. Outside St. Margarets, Westminster

The Oxford crew at my parents' house, March 1923

splendid histrionic display. The thought of dear Nannos sprinting across the Struma swamps madly waving his sword was somewhat incongruous. I'm glad to say we were well-mannered enough to appear to take his explanation absolutely seriously. We didn't even smile. Awe and admiration were written on our faces. Someone asked him how his scabbard came by its kink, thinking we should be regaled with some absorbing tale of derring-do. His reply came as something of an anti-climax. "Oh, zat?" he remarked casually, "a mule stepped on it."

The next day I was detailed to show my sector of the line to a party of his sword-following troops. They were a wild and woolly lot, some of them sporting long black beards. There was really nothing to show them. The only sign of any sort of military preparation were three ancient and overgrown redoubts, spaced at intervals of about twenty yards, backed by a shallow inter-communicating trench. It was difficult to understand why they had ever been constructed. Breathing down my neck, with blood lust in their eyes, the Greek troops followed me into the first redoubt. There was absolutely nothing to say and, even if there had been, the language difficulty would have proved insurmountable. By their grunts and signs it was obvious that they wished to be told the particular form of activity to which each redoubt was allotted. In the first redoubt I grasped an imaginary machine gun and exclaimed, "Bang, bang, bang, bang, bang!" In the second I went through some bomb-throwing mime, whilst in the third I took careful aim with an odd strip of wood I found lying at my feet and pulled an imaginary trigger. I felt I had surmounted a tricky situation with some credit. By their intense concentration I knew my explanations had been absorbed. They were obviously delighted.

In a day or two we packed our kit and set forth for the Vardar. We bivouacked one night on the way. Why one of the steep sides of a ravine was chosen as a suitable encampment I shall never understand. We spent a disturbed night. This was due neither to our own nor enemy activity, but to the gradient of our sleeping quarters. When lying prone one felt almost that one was standing upright, and no sooner had we dozed off than we started slipping down the sides of the ravine; only by crawling on hands and knees could we regain the comparative shelter of the bivouac.

On the way up to the line our route lay directly in front of one of our battery positions. As our battalion arrived on the scene, a nearby battery started to shell the enemy lines. Our colonel sent me ahead to find out how long we could expect the straffe to last, "Only keep low and don't get your head in front of a gun." I did as I was bid and eventually found my way into a dugout, where a few officers were sitting around with glasses in their hands. The comparative quiet of the dugout contrasted strangely with the thunder of the guns outside.

"Have a drink, old boy."
"How long are we going on?"
"Oh, we shall have finished our night's work in a minute or two."

Having arrived at our destination, we found ourselves quartered in another ravine some few miles to the rear of the Vardar front. The following day our company commander, with his platoon commanders, rode up to the front line to get the general lie of the land. On our way back a violent rainstorm broke; in order to avoid the muddy spate pouring down the trenches leading down to the lines I levered myself up on to the side of the trench, and slipped and gashed my knee severely on a sharp stone protruding from the side of the trench. My ride back to base, with the gash on my knee opening and shutting as I rode, was very far from comfortable, though much to my relief it showed no signs of turning septic.

One day I found and befriended a young hawk which seemed somewhat the worse for wear. My batman found a cage of ample proportions, and from then on most of my spare time was spent in catching locusts with which to assuage its seemingly insatiable appetite. When eventually we moved up into the line I realized that to go hunting for locusts in no-man's-land, with the Bulgars entrenched some two or three hundred yards away, might be misunderstood;

HUNTING IN NO-MAN'S-LAND

and as the hawk was by that time fully restored to health, I let it go.

The Bulgars' idea of warfare could not be termed aggressive nor was it very imaginative. They lobbed over three or four shells at about five o'clock every evening. They invariably landed in approximately the same spot. It was a simple matter therefore to avoid lingering there at that particular time. At night they fired a few pip squeaks. One could trace their path as they ricocheted along the ground towards our lines. Beyond that they did little but fire an occasional Verey light, again invariably from the same spot. We endured a week of the most fearful monotony before moving up into the line. There we found Bulgars' trenches were some two or three hundred yards away. I was given a dugout hewn out of solid rock, so my danger even should the enemy have scored a direct hit was minimal. Its only drawback was that it was infested with rats. I procured some traps and was successful in reducing the rat population to normal proportions. There was little enemy activity. Our own artillery was far from inactive. We were not always happy with their marksmanship, especially one evening when they scored a direct hit on one of our dugouts. A few fiery words were exchanged on the telephone and all was peace and quiet again.

The Bulgar line had one great advantage over ours. It included the Black Rock, which protruded some fifty or sixty feet into the air. By dint of tunnelling into this natural fortress from behind, the Bulgars had formed a well-nigh impregnable position. It was scarred by several direct hits from our artillery and it was said that when one of these occurred you could hear the occupants dissolve into gales of derisory laughter.

Our diet consisted almost exclusively of tinned salmon. The company cook was given instructions that he must find at least five different ways of serving it. It didn't matter if it looked the same but somehow or other by the liberal use of curry powder or the addition of a couple of tablespoons of vinegar it had to be given a different taste. We drank whisky of doubtful origin and an extremely effervescent brew of

Japanese beer. I was lucky in having a wonderful batman who had formerly acted in that capacity to Albert Ball, V.C., the indomitable flying ace who had met his death on the Western Front. Langley acted as mother, father and nanny to me for so long as we were together. He could conjure water from God knows where, so that I could erect my canvas hip bath and occasionally enjoy the luxury of a thorough good soak in my dugout.

The line of our trenches took some peculiar twists and turns. One night a sentry reported that he had noticed a good deal of movement in the Bulgar trenches. He indicated the direction from which it had come. I told him not to worry. The movement he had spotted emanated from one of our own companies on our left flank.

After a few days in the trenches I concluded that I must make a reconnaissance in no-man's-land. There was no possible object in such a manœuvre, but somehow or other I felt that I had to show my platoon that I was completely fearless, which was very far from being the case. Having warned my platoon against challenging anyone for the next half hour, I crawled over the top with my sergeant, who knew the gaps in the barbed wire entanglements. As we slithered along on our bellies I couldn't help thinking what a pointless exercise it was. We were not very inquisitive and never ventured very near the Bulgar lines. Suddenly from one of our own sentries there came a clear bell-like challenge, "Who goes there?" We hissed back, "Shut up, you bloody fool. It's your platoon commander and sergeant. For God's sake keep your mouth shut." Eventually we returned to our lines. For the first time I realized how fortunate I was to be in the Middle East. On the Western Front I imagined that crawling about in a maze of barbed wire was a nightly occurrence.

As I went the rounds of my sector at night, I came to the conclusion that, should I meet any Bulgars, by the time I had unbuttoned my holster, drawn and cocked my revolver, I should be a dead man. I therefore rather stupidly took to going around with an unbuttoned holster and my revolver fully cocked. One evening after returning to my dugout

I stooped down to pick up a writing pad, when my revolver slipped out of the holster, fell to the ground and went off. I glanced to my left and noted a hole in my mosquito net. I reckoned that the bullet must have passed an inch or so from my head. Langley who had just left me ran back, "Thank God, you're alive, sir! M'heart was in m'mooth. M'heart was in m'mooth!" It was certainly a near thing. Had it proved fatal, I suppose it would have been assumed that I couldn't take it and had taken the easiest way out.

One day we were visited by our colonel, who remarked, "Oh by the way, Nickalls, you're going on a course down at the base." I received this information with mixed feelings. If they felt I was woefully undertrained they were absolutely right. Had I made any glaring errors? I didn't think so. Certainly I had never been told about them. Did they want to get rid of me? I couldn't really believe that, I seemed to have got on well with all and sundry. I didn't ask any questions and concluded that I'd better stop worrying about it.

Two days later the course was inaugurated by General Milne—the Commander-in-Chief. This was August 1918 and he informed us that things were going well for the Allied armies. He could give no promises of the war being over in one or two months, but added that from now on everything should go very much in our favour. This was heartening news.

In about three days' time I began to feel pretty queer. I reported to the M.O. who told me to go back to bed. The next morning, feeling even worse, I reported again, only to be greeted with "Hallo, Nickalls, I thought I cured you yesterday!" I returned to bed feeling as bad as ever. I realized that something was very wrong. To make matters worse, a party of boisterous drunks who were sharing my tent returned late at night and started to kick up a hell of a noise. I pleaded for a little less din only to be greeted with, "D'you hear that, boys. This chap says he's ill. Not only ill but damned ill." Gales of laughter followed this sally. The next morning I suffered a severe shivering attack followed by a bout of vomiting and my temperature soared. The M.O.

visited me the next morning, diagnosed malignant malaria and packed me off to hospital. After a jolting journey of some three hours I found myself in a marquee together with some thirty others. My condition was considered to be sufficiently serious for a cable to be sent to my parents to the effect that I was on the danger list.

The hospital was manned entirely by Australian nurses — absolute darlings who never spared themselves on our behalf. The matron in charge, though quite young, certainly had the instincts of the grande dame. She went her rounds once every twenty-four hours attended by three or four of her staff, subdued and discreetly humble. No suggestion of sunlight penetrated the ward yet she never lowered her white silk parasol. I concluded that its uses were symbolic rather than functional. I suppose I was her youngest patient and when she arrived at my bedside she invariably greeted me with the words, "Well, how's the babe this evening?"

I don't know how much advance has since been made in the treatment of malaria. In those days it was quinine and still more quinine. Its taste was foul and I never got used to it. Not content with administering it orally they would make a hole in your thigh and pour in quantities of the beastly stuff for good measure. I suppose it did a certain amount of good, though the only effects of which one was conscious were deafness accompanied by a singing in the ears. I think it impaired one mentally as well. Sometimes they treated me to a glass of champagne. The first time they gave me a glass of port I mistook it for gravy and poured it over some meat which passed for mutton. I'm bound to say the flavour was greatly improved. The only disturbance at nights was the march of the burial squads whose route ran close to our marquee. My days were constantly disrupted by bouts of severe malarial attacks. Invariably they followed the same course, shivering, vomiting and then the onslaught of raging fever. This was the most unpleasant part of the proceedings. What a relief when one suddenly started to sweat copiously! Pints of liquid poured from my body. My bedclothes became a sodden tangled mass. At last one was rubbed down, and weak but happy, snuggled into the welcome embrace of clean dry sheets. Day followed day. I really had no idea of how long I had been there. At last I was told I could dress and go out for a short stroll. Outside I felt so pleased with my recovery that I broke into a little jog-trot. There was a sudden pain in my knees. What on earth was it? I tried looking down at my knees as I ran. It was then that I noticed that my knees were knocking together. I hadn't realized I was quite so weak.

Within a week our revolvers and such ammunition as we had were called in and we were told that we could collect them on our return to London. We embarked on a hospital ship. Two Spanish observers sailed with us. They were there to guarantee that the ship was completely unarmed. At night two enormous red crosses were picked out in electric lights on either side of the vessel while two bands of green lights encircled the ship. We were bound it seemed for Malta. No untoward incident disturbed our journey, but on one occasion the ship's warning hooters sent us scurrying for our life jackets. We waited in vain for the crump and shudder of a torpedo to strike us. Nothing happened, and then cocking an eye towards the wake of our ship we realized we were turning round. It appeared that one of our passengers with a cry of "come on, boys" had dived into the Mediterranean. When we first spotted him, he was about half a mile from us swimming strongly in our direction. A lifeboat put out and hauled him aboard. As he stepped back on to the ship to the cheers of the ship's company an N.C.O. clapped a hand on his shoulder. It looked very much as though he was for detention; whereas, of course, being obviously a mental case, the sick bay would have been a far more suitable destination.

My active service had come to an end. Perhaps it would be more accurate to describe it as my "inactive service". I look back on it now and realize how utterly useless I had been, and what a hell of a lot of money I had cost the country. I never fired a shot in anger. In fact I was quite overcome with a sense of hopeless inadequacy, which was depressing to say the least of it.

Chapter 7

Home Sweet Home?

Our hospital ship dropped anchor in Valetta harbour and we dawdled away some ten weeks on Malta, where we celebrated the Armistice. It was, however, a welcome moment when we learned that we should be home in time for Christmas and in early December we embarked for Taranto.

Our sea crossing to Taranto proved a very rough passage. We were now no longer emblazoned as a hospital ship and the heat of my cabin was insupportable. On my asking for the porthole to be opened, I was told that this was not in order in case I showed a light, although it was over a month since the Armistice had been declared. The porthole was fastened by a nut screwed very securely. I saw a suffocating night ahead of me. Somehow I had to devise a spanner to open the porthole. I tied the ends of two walking sticks together so that their ferrules were about an inch apart. Carefully turning off the light I applied my make-do spanner to the crucial nut holding the porthole and to my intense relief it worked and a gust of gloriously fresh air filled the cabin. I never turned the light on and spent a comfortable night. I was rather proud of this ludicrously simple ruse. The more so because I am completely unmechanically minded. In Macedonia, I had lectured on the Lewis gun, though in fact I had never grasped exactly how it worked.

In Taranto I was put to bed with one of my recurring malarial bouts. Three beds from mine a man was dying of pneumonia. It was a harrowing experience to hear his suffering, though when I thought of all the other ghastly nightmares others had endured I counted myself extremely fortunate. His breathing became more and more congested, his babblings less and less coherent. Summoning all my powers of concentration, I buried myself in a book (*Peg Wuffington*). After an hour's hard reading I paused. No longer was there that ghastly fighting for breath. I thanked God that the poor fellow's sufferings were at an end.

In a few days we entrained for the long return journey through Italy and France. We started at an extremely leisurely pace. We reckoned that at one time we took exactly twelve hours to cover sixteen miles. In a day or so we were skirting the seaboard of the Italian and French Rivieras. Our spirits rose, the journey became welcome and invigorating. Eventually we reached the coast and crossed the Channel. I was marked down as a stretcher case. On our way to London the word went round that stretcher cases would not be allowed Christmas leave. The date was December 20th. Descending from the train, dutifully I lay down on a waiting stretcher and was being carried up the platform when I asked my bearers to put me down. I told them that if they had been ordered to carry their stretcher to a waiting ambulance I would not deter them, but I preferred to walk. I got up and marched along the platform whilst the bearers doggedly walked alongside me. As I climbed into the ambulance they turned round and marched off still bearing an empty stretcher. I waved them goodbye. To the best of their ability they had carried out their orders and to my great relief I could no longer be branded as a "stretcher case".

I was given the choice of a hospital in Reading or Oxford. I chose Oxford and that evening found myself ensconced in a comfortable bed in Somerville College, which at that time had been converted into a hospital. I was within three or four hundred yards of St. John's where I had been quartered some twelve months previously. The next morning my parents called for me in a hired car and I was given Christmas leave.

In a few weeks I returned to the Isle of Sheppey, which seemed to be as dreary as ever except that everyone was clamouring for demobilization. No sooner had I settled down again than we were moved up to Rugeley in Staffordshire. Everyone was fed to the back teeth and seemed to take liberties that they would never have contemplated prior to the Armistice. As an example, I was supervising the serving of the men's dinner one day when one of them shouted, "Call that an effing dinner? I'll fling the bloody stuff in your face in a minute." "Take that man's name," I said to the sergeant. In the orderly room the next day I was asked how I knew he was addressing me. "Well," I replied, "as he was only six feet from me when he said it, I think he was taking an unwarranted risk." Twenty-eight days' detention was the sentence. I was sorry for him. The food wasn't particularly appetizing, yet somehow I don't feel that a suggestion from me that the commissariat of the whole battalion needed a shake-up would have made any difference.

Each officer had a cubicle to himself, with a solid fuel stove and an enamel chamber pot. On March 31st some of us stayed drinking in the Mess until after midnight. Suddenly we realized it was All Fool's Day. What could we do? We would pay a visit to every one of our colleagues in the battalion, and carefully avoiding the C.O., the major and the adjutant, we opened every officer's door, walked in and announced, "It's April Fools' Day", whereupon we picked up their jerry and placed it on top of the stove. The resultant stench when the contents came to the boil must have been overwhelming. We went our rounds amidst gales of uncontrollable laughter. This to us was the merriest prank that had ever been devised. It was only in after years that I began to realize how terribly unfunny it all was. The sheer idiocy of the whole performance shames me, reminding me so much of that couplet of G. K. Chesterton's:

> My friends, we will not go again or ape an ancient rage,
> Or stretch the folly of our youth to be the shame of age.

Eventually my demobilization papers came through. How thankful I was. I went before a medical board who awarded me a pension of some eighty odd pounds for the first year, which was reduced to forty pounds a year later, which proved to be my final compensation. I wasn't displeased nor did I think it stingy. At that time I was only too glad of it. Our fare was paid to any point in the British Isles we might choose. Usually one picked the point nearest one's home. This was not invariably the case and I was full of admiration for a colleague of mine who felt that a bird-watching holiday might not come amiss. To this end he picked the most northerly point in Scotland from which to take leave of the army.

As I have previously recorded I agreed with my father that I should delay for a year any attempt to enter Oxford. By that time, if all went well, I should have thrown off my bouts of recurring malaria. As luck would have it Roger Eckersley, with whom at a later date I was destined to become more closely acquainted, informed me that they were looking for decipherers in the Foreign Office. It required no specialized knowledge and, having sworn an oath that I would divulge nothing, I was duly installed in a large airy room overlooking the Horse Guards Parade, with about ten others engaged on the same duties. I stayed there for about nine months and enjoyed every minute of it. We were warned not to leave any confidential papers lying about. It was darkly rumoured that during the war someone had on his desk a half-deciphered message giving the order in which the German Navy was sailing forth into the North Sea for an action which culminated in the Battle of Jutland. This luckless decipherer had left the room for a moment to find on his return that both his half-deciphered message together with the original had disappeared — a grisly tale.

"R" was the cipher commonly used for the less important messages. It had been in use for so long that it was assumed that it was known the world over. Even at a distance of over fifty years I can remember that 4131 signified "full stop. New paragraph", and that 1832 signified "London". I never quite grasped why, if the code was so well known, they went to the bother of transmitting the message by cipher at all. One occupant of our room, I never knew his initials but his name was Antrobus, had a phenomenal knowledge of "R", and his memory was astonishing. I was credibly informed that at one Foreign Office dinner he made a speech in cipher "R" which was well understood by the majority of his audience.

It was at this time that any message concerning Russia was apt to contain various references to the "lefts", the "rights" or even on occasions the "outside rights". As far as I was concerned it sounded as though it were an account of a soccer match. One of the occupants of our room—Reggie Hooper, afterwards to become editor of the *Bystander* and *Tatler*, was a man of a quiet and dry humour. He wrote a brilliant satire of the type of dispatches which were coming through at that time. After an introductory sentence, it continued, "The outside lefts are, if I may say so, determined not to be left outside", and it finished, "Summing up the position I would suggest that via media should be the principal plank in the platform of his opponents."

My father had chosen, as one of my godfathers, a close rowing friend of his in whose company he had been successful in the Oxford and Cambridge Boat Race, as well as in the pair-oared race at Henley Regatta—the Goblets. A more kindly and solicitous godfather it would be hard to imagine. In his earlier years he had been Governor of Madras, and in that capacity had obviously known the workings of the Foreign Office. He was elated at my employment and jumped to the conclusion that I intended to make it a whole time job. It was most unlikely that they would ever have accepted me and even had they done so, I felt it was not my job. I had overheard a conversation in connection with expenses which went something like this:

"Says he's spent over £200 of his own money on the mission."
"What's he grumbling about? He's had a jolly good trip, hasn't he?"

Obviously a private income was virtually an essential, and this ruled me out.

My malaria had ceased its regular periodic attacks and the hope of entering Magdalen College, Oxford, for the summer term of 1920 loomed ahead. I realized that I should have to take a college entry examination before going into residence. I wrote to a former don of the College, my old friend Charles

HOME SWEET HOME?

Fletcher, asking for any advice as to the books I should be studying. He did all he could to set me on the right path and ended his letter "between you and me the present lot of dons at Magdalen are the most appalling lot of mokes unhung. Only don't tell them I said so."

Chapter 8

No, No, They Can't Take That Away From Me

IN his autobiography *The Last Enemy* Richard Hilary, one of those dauntless Battle of Britain pilots, writes, "I went up to Oxford with the intention of rowing myself into the Sudan Civil Service — that race of blacks ruled by 'blues'."

It would be ludicrous to pretend that I had any ambition to enter that service, though looking back, and noting the number of rowing blues they employed over the years, it would seem that prowess at rowing was a strong influence in the choice of suitable candidates. I had a burning desire to excel at rowing, though not as a means to any particular end. I just wanted to be good at something. I knew only too well that I was still suffering from an inferiority complex — a hangover from my Eton days — and I thought that some success, in however humble a way, might go some way to eradicating this mental burden.

My acceptance by Magdalen, I thought, should not prove too difficult. Having regard to my war service, I thought they would be lenient when it came to taking my college entrance examination, even though I had failed to pass my School Certificate some years previously. My rowing friends who were already up at Magdalen encouraged me in the belief that there would be no difficulty and that the whole thing was just a matter of form. They explained there would be no room for me in the College itself and advised me to book "digs". This I proceeded to do. They went further than this and asked me to row in the College eight, which they hoped would go Head of the River.

As soon as I arrived in Oxford I took the College entrance

NO, NO, THEY CAN'T TAKE THAT AWAY FROM ME

exam. Even the fact that the papers were far beyond my capabilities didn't worry me a great deal. I felt it would all come right in the end. Whilst waiting for the results I continued practising in the College eight every afternoon.

And then the blow fell. I had "failed to satisfy the examiners". There were some ugly rumours to the effect that there were eleven vacancies and out of some forty-eight candidates I had been placed forty-sixth. A polite note asked me to call on the President of Magdalen, Sir Herbert Warren. I kept the appointment. In his quiet, gentle way, Warren expressed his great regret that they were unable to accept me. Something dramatic was called for. Here was something I had set my heart on. Something that I knew instinctively would affect my whole future was being brutally snatched from me at the last moment. I burst into tears and sobbed my heart out. How much of this was genuine and how much histrionic I have never been able to decide. Was it a last despairing ploy? My final gambit? Honestly I don't know. My father had himself been an undergraduate under the Presidency of Warren and had remained on the best of terms with him. He, however, was in America at this particular moment. My mother, poor soul, did her best. She wrote to Warren promising him that should he take me he would never regret it.

To return to the interview, Warren hesitated and then in the same sympathetic tone of voice remarked, "Of course, I can't help feeling flattered that you want to come up to Magdalen so much. I'll see what I can do." I had to wait a week for the decision of the tutorial board — the longest week I ever remember. And then, what blessed relief, the tutorial board came to the conclusion that they had not made sufficient allowance for my war service. In fact they had changed their mind — I was in. I had never before felt so happy.

The traditional scholastic curriculum did not apply to those who could claim an experience of active service. S. G. Lee, a greatly beloved Magdalen don, was to be my tutor. A brief discussion with him decided that my first year was to be given over to the taking of an economic diploma and, should I succeed in that endeavour, I could make up my mind what I should read in order to obtain a degree. I believe I am correct in saying that at Cambridge a degree was awarded for economics though at Oxford at that time it merited no more than a diploma. Within a week I was busy with the teachings of Adam Smith. Ricardo's Theory of Rent seemed to claim a good deal more of my attention than I felt it deserved. My choice of two special subjects ended in my selection of *Malthus on the Population* and *The Economics of Transport*. I soon discovered that the perusal of past papers taken by students of economics was of tremendous assistance.

It didn't take long to realize that one could have known *Malthus on the Population* almost by heart and still have failed dismally in that particular subject. Past papers revealed that it wasn't so much a knowledge of the book which was required, as of what other authorities had written about the book. I attended lectures regularly and worked hard, realizing that failure to take my diploma would almost certainly have led to my being "sent down", thus depriving me of my last two years at the university. It appeared that there were only two of us in the College studying economics, Ivor Churchill and myself, and every week we submitted an essay on a set subject to our tutor, Luggins — the undergraduates' affectionate rendering of S. G. Lee. At the beginning of the summer term, 1921, I realized that we should be sitting for our diploma in June. One day, some six weeks before our ordeal, Ivor Churchill enquired casually the exact date of the examination. I mentioned the date. His face revealed some concern at this news. "I can't possibly sit on that day," he replied. "I'm going to the Derby. I shall get a doctor's certificate to the effect that I'm not well enough to sit." This he managed to obtain, seemingly with some ease.

I sat for and obtained my diploma. Churchill did not seem to be amongst the candidates. The following week I attended my weekly tutorial and noting his absence I asked what had happened to him. "He's not very fit," came the reply. "We've advised him to go down and not come up again until his health has improved." Needless to say he

My mother with her youngest son Rodney (far right) and two other pupils from Cothill

The author in rowing kit (1921)

Henley Regatta, Finals Day. L. to R. The Prime Minister Mr. Stanley Baldwin, Prince Henry of Gloucester, Lord Desborough and Mr. Harcourt G. Gold walking along the towing path

Oxford and Cambridge Boat Race. Commentaries by G. O. Nickalls and J. C. Squire from the launch *Magician* with engineers in foreground. This was the first running commentary of a Boat Race

NO, NO, THEY CAN'T TAKE THAT AWAY FROM ME

took the hint and never came back into residence. I was sorry. I had found him a charming, agreeable companion. I never saw him again and I suspect that the college authorities realized that our examination fell on a very "inconvenient" date.

The question of how my university education was to be paid for was a matter of some moment to me. My father, shoving and string-pulling, had at the age of fifty pushed his way into the army and had seen service in France. I suspected he was about as hard up as I was. Ever since I was a small boy I had been urged to be thrifty. Every tip I received went into a money box. By the time I was twenty-one I had amassed the princely sum of £250. In addition to this I was fortunate enough to be awarded a university grant of £17 a term.

I therefore approached my father and told him that from a financial point of view he need not worry for at least a year. My grant, together with my life's savings, would see me through. After that — well, we would have to see. For my second year I had to rely on paternal assistance. Whether I could rely on him for a third year was extremely doubtful. Unbeknown to me, my father approached the directors of the wine merchants W. & A. Gilbey, of which my maternal grandfather had been an original partner. Nobly they clubbed together and produced a sum which saw me comfortably through my last year. I have never ceased to be grateful to these generous relatives for their much needed assistance. I only hope they had no cause to regret their generosity.

As my name is inclined to be connected with rowing, that first glorious summer at Oxford is perhaps worthy of mention not as proof of my own prowess, but rather as an indication of my good fortune in being associated with so many outstanding oarsmen. As anticipated, Magdalen went Head of the River, and a week or so later R. S. C. Lucas and I were successful in winning the university pair-oared race. In preparation for Henley Regatta E. D. Horsfall who, as an oarsman, had made a distinguished name for himself prior to the war, came in as stroke. This

A RAINBOW IN THE SKY

made us into a really good crew. We won the Grand Challenge Cup at Henley with some ease. There was not much competition that year (1920) and Lucas and myself were successful in the Goblets.

The Olympic Games were being held in Antwerp that year, and a crew to represent the United Kingdom was to be sent. At that time there was what amounted to a tacit understanding that, when it came to international representation, a Leander crew should be picked. What guided the authorities in this particular piece of folly I have never been able to understand, except perhaps the fact that a Leander crew had been successful in the eight-oared Olympic events of 1908 and 1912. On this occasion they took five men from the Magdalen crew and called upon three Leander men to, in their opinion, "strengthen" us. Not content with this, the selectors made the captain of Leander the captain of the newly formed crew. This was a piece of unforgivable stupidity. Horsfall, to whom the four other Magdalen men were devoted, was a born leader, who with his experience and reputation, as well as by his instinctive handling of men, exercised a tremendous influence on the crew. The deposing of him as captain was bound to lead to friction, as indeed it did.

The organization of these Olympics, so far as rowing was concerned, was quite appalling. On arrival, we discovered that the rowing took place on a canal outside Brussels. We were accommodated there in a station hotel which could not provide training food, added to which we had a lengthy and dusty tram journey to the course and back every day. For our first outing we had to retrieve our boat from a truck on a railway siding and carry it for well over a mile through the countryside of Belgium to the boat house. The American Navy crew, who were representing the United States, were ensconced in their own quarters close to the course, had made their own catering arrangements and had been in residence there for some weeks prior to our arrival. We met them in the final and it proved a race I am unlikely to forget. We maintained a high rate of striking yet, as is always the case when a crew is perfectly synchronized, we seemed to have plenty of time. It was all so smooth, powerful and effective. Gradually we established an encouraging lead, if we could only keep this going we must win. It was a glorious feeling. We were now three-quarters of a length ahead. Could we clear them and make certain of victory? We were still going well but the Americans with a considerable advantage in weight were hanging on; fighting every inch of the way. About two minutes from the finish they started to put on the pressure. I didn't look at them, that would have been to jeopardize my time-keeping, but I could see them out of the corner of my eye. We made herculean efforts to stave off their attack. Inexorably they gained. There was only a hundred yards to go. They were alongside us, and with a bare fifteen seconds left they took the lead for the first time and got home by 4/5th of a second — in distance about six feet.

That was the fastest crew in which I ever had the privilege of performing. My best chance of ever winning a gold medal. Had we been allowed to remain as a college crew we might easily have done it. Had our own organization been anything but pathetic we might have succeeded. To overcome both obstacles was beyond us.

Jack Beresford, to my mind the finest sculler from this country I ever saw in action, was the only other British entry at that Regatta. He suffered a similar fate, being beaten by one second by the American, J. B. Kelly (the father of Princess Grace of Monaco). Beresford's triumph was however merely delayed, for amongst many other Olympic medals he won the single sculls in the 1924 Olympics in Paris.

Back at Oxford the following term I stroked the Magdalen crew which won the university fours. I was excused Trial Eights as it was felt that I had proved myself sufficiently to warrant my inclusion in the Oxford crew of the following year. This was the only rest I had from the river during my three years and one term up at Oxford.

Chapter 9

"Ship Money, You Bloody Fool!"

I WAS determined to make the most of my time at Oxford. I would dearly have loved to be auditioned for a part in the annual production of the O.U.D.S. (Oxford University Dramatic Society). Such a dream was never to be realized. It was a matter of conflicting dates. The O.U.D.S. went into rehearsal at the beginning of the Spring Term — a time when men dedicated to the river were busy with their own rehearsals for the Oxford and Cambridge Boat Race. The O.U.D.S. choice for 1921 was *Anthony and Cleopatra*. It was customary to ask a professional to play the leading lady, and that year Cathleen Nesbitt accepted the part of Cleopatra. Anthony was played by Cecil Ramage — a man with exceptional good looks and an imposing stature. This partnership was the prelude to their marriage. I met him only once. During my first term he arrived at my lodgings in the "High" and asked me if I would coach his college crew, which happened to be Pembroke. I was greatly flattered but had, nevertheless, to decline.

In my last year Gerald Gardiner, afterwards to become Lord Chancellor, had enlisted the services of J. B. Fagan as producer. They were playing *Henry IV, Part I*. Apparently that year was an anniversary of the foundation of the O.U.D.S., and as *Henry IV, Part I* had been their opening production it was felt that a repetition would be appropriate. I attended one or two rehearsals and came away full of admiration for the sheer dexterity and professionalism with which Fagan handled his cast. With his finals in prospect Gerald Gardiner was unable to play in this production. He did however speak a prologue quite

"SHIP MONEY, YOU BLOODY FOOL!"

beautifully. It had been written for the occasion by Fagan himself and contained the pun "... trailing O.U.D.S. of glory".

Some two years later Jack Hulbert and Cecily Courtneidge brought a revue *Pot Luck* to Oxford. Bobby Howes, at that time a promising youngster, was in the cast. One evening I attended a breezy talk which Hulbert gave to the O.U.D.S. and was introduced to him afterwards. He accepted an invitation for himself and his wife to lunch with me in my rooms in College the next day. In the middle of luncheon Jack Hulbert remarked quite casually that he was pretty sure that his father had been captain of the Magdalen College Boat Club way back in the seventies. I thought this most unlikely, remembering that he himself had been up at Cambridge. "If you care to stroll down to the College Barge this afternoon we'll have a look," I said. "Photographs of all our former captains are hanging there." After a glass of port we all walked down to the Barge and in a matter of seconds he was pointing to an oval photograph. "That's him," he exclaimed, and there sure enough below it was the name Hulbert. I could see at once there was a strong family likeness; the only difference being that the man in the photograph sported a luxuriant Victorian moustache. It was just the sort of moustache that Jack Hulbert himself used when playing one of his low-life comedy sketches. The resemblance was quite remarkable.

I appeared only once on the stage at Oxford. It occurred to someone to revive the Magdalen Amateur Dramatic Society. On many matters concerning undergraduate activities the advice was sought of a very remarkable college servant. There is no one who was at Magdalen during these years who will not remember Mr. Gynes. He was responsible for the construction of a golf course in the purlieus of Cowley, and was himself no mean performer. I am not certain whether he played down to scratch but he certainly had a very low handicap. His general knowledge was encyclopaedic and one of his passions in life was the stage. He had a remarkable collection of programmes of every single play he had ever attended. He knew who had played who in almost any production of the last forty years. You couldn't floor him. Who was the first negro to play Othello? Gynes knew. It was therefore obvious that when the revival of the Dramatic Society was first mooted, Gynes should be consulted. It was he who realized that to combine the aesthetic and sporting elements within the college, a president who had his feet, so to speak, in both camps should be chosen. To him I appeared to fulfil these qualifications. Someone asked me if I would take it on and I accepted with alacrity. In the Magdalen Junior Commonroom we gave a number of performances and on the final curtain made a collection for the Eton Mission.

Ours was a triple bill. Sir Gyles Isham, just up from Rugby, played the Bishop in *The Bishop's Candlesticks*. Later he was to become President of the O.U.D.S., and on going down he took up the stage as a career. It still gives me a certain satisfaction to recall that the very first time he trod the boards at Oxford it was under my auspices. With Alfred Tennyson d'Eyncourt I played a duologue by Arthur Wimperis—*The Eternal Triangle*. This was a short curtain raiser dealing almost exclusively with marital infidelity—and in those days considered extremely risqué.

I was never a member of the Union, my powers of debate being negligible. However, I attended one memorable evening when Winston Churchill had agreed to speak. Beverley Nichols was President. It was he who had initiated the wearing of buttonholes of cerise carnations by officers of the Union. The motion was "That this House deplores the continuance of the Coalition Government". I had been told that Winston Churchill was at his best when heckled. We were not to be disappointed. Towards the end of his speech he remarked, "And now we come to Ireland." Immediately there were cries of, "Take your troops away, sir! Take your troops away." Without a moment's hesitation he flashed back: "That a great country like England, having just emerged from a victorious war, should be hustled. . . . I say hustled out of its own Dominions by a lot of low, lying, scurrilous rogues. It's ridiculous, gentlemen. It's ridiculous." I can't remember whether or no the House did deplore the

"SHIP MONEY, YOU BLOODY FOOL!"

continuance of the Coalition. I remember however that it was a thoroughly entertaining evening.

Within a few weeks of writing the above I met Beverley Nichols at an evening party. I repeated to him my recollection of that evening and asked him if his remembrance of it was the same as mine. "The gist of your version is perfectly correct," he replied. "Though the epithets he applied were not 'low-lying, scurrilous rogues', but 'footpads and assassins'. I remember very well," he continued, "because he had breakfast with me the next day and asked me if he had said anything he shouldn't." "Well, sir," replied Beverley Nichols. "You did call them 'footpads and assassins'." "Did I?" enquired Churchill laconically. "Oh that's all right."

Having been in residence at Magdalen before the First World War the Prince of Wales (afterwards the Duke of Windsor) paid a visit to his old college. With some half-dozen other members of the college I was invited by Warren to a luncheon given in the Prince's honour. During a pause in the conversation, the subject of lady undergraduates was mentioned. "Nickalls has a cousin up at St. Hugh's," remarked Warren. Looking down the table the Prince enquired, "Is she very ugly?" What could I say? A certain amount of family loyalty seemed to be called for. "Brutalized by games," I ventured. In ordinary circumstances I should have been quite pleased with this particular parry if only it had been original. It wasn't. I had heard it applied to quite another lady but a few days previously.

Lunch over, we were ushered into the President's study. A visitors' book lay ominously on the table. It was ordained that the signature of His Royal Highness should occupy one whole page to itself whilst the remainder of the party appended theirs on the opposite page. "Would you sign the Visitors' Book?" enquired Warren. I must say the remark sounded more like a command than a request. His Royal Highness couldn't resist a little tease. Winking at the other guests, he said, "I don't think I want to sign that. After all I've signed it before, haven't I?" Warren was not to be denied. "I think we should like you to sign it again," he murmured. It was obvious he had set his heart on it, so his royal guest did as he was bid.

When a college distinguishes itself by winning the inter-college cricket or rugby cup, or going Head of the River, such an event is invariably celebrated by a bump supper followed by a bonfire. In my day these suppers were functions to be remembered. High spirits accompanied by a good deal of noise were much in evidence. After dinner speeches went on for hours. Each speaker emphasized how wonderfully everyone had performed except himself, and praised the tremendous encouragement and support received from the college. How the captain had been a tower of strength and without him . . . etc. etc. etc. Each speech seemed to be exactly the same, and even if a speaker happened to make an original or amusing remark (a very rare occurrence) the whole point of the sally was lost in the general hubbub.

A bonfire of noble proportions was always prepared in one of the quads, and as soon as we staggered befuzzled from the college hall it was ceremoniously lighted; whereupon every member of the college screamed, shouted and pranced like dancing dervishes until the last embers had died away. How the surrounding college buildings were not burnt to the ground has always mystified me.

Years after I had gone down I was watching these junketings with George Gordon who, by that time, had succeeded Warren as President. The bonfire in that particular year had been built in an open space. The college authorities had obviously realized the dangers which had formerly threatened the college buildings. "You have noticed no doubt," remarked Gordon, "that an extraordinary number of packing cases are being thrown on to the fire. Quite deliberately we have scattered some thirty or forty of them within a two hundred yard radius of the fire. Purely a precautionary measure. We came to the conclusion that so long as the wilder spirits in the college could find plenty of timber to feed the flames, some of the college's more valuable possessions would stand a greater chance of survival." I had to admit that this was pretty shrewd reasoning.

"SHIP MONEY, YOU BLOODY FOOL!"

Some years later I had been coaching a Magdalen crew and the college were celebrating their Head of the River triumph in the usual way. Suddenly a friend came up from behind me. "You see our college giant over there. Keep well clear of him. He has a nasty habit of gripping his victims round their shoulders and walking them backwards into the bonfire. It can be damn dangerous I assure you." I saw the so-called giant—a man not far short of seven foot and of herculean proportions. A trial of strength would obviously be useless. He was at the height of his powers whilst I was over fifty. I intended to keep a wary eye on him. Alas, my mind was distracted for a moment and—oh horrors—I found myself in the grip of this drink-crazy monster. What should I do? Luckily his coat was open in front and as he started to push me backwards towards the bonfire I realized I must act quickly. Without putting up too much resistance I felt hurriedly up and down his stomach until I found his navel. With lightning speed I inserted my thumbs in the appropriate aperture, drove them right home until they were well and truly embedded in his stomach, then pulled them apart with all my strength. The result astonished even me. My ruse succeeded beyond my wildest dreams. I was staggered. He was staggered too. He released his hold and went rolling all over the place screaming, "That chap has practically ripped out my navel." He kept well away from me for the rest of the evening. One or two of my friends who had watched the episode, came up in wonderment and joy. "What on earth did you do to him?" they asked. "No one's ever got the better of him before." "Oh, nothing," I replied blandly, "I just happen to be a little stronger that's all."

Having obtained my Economic Diploma I decided, for no very good reason, that I would sit for an Honours Degree in History. I should be able to do this in two years, providing the cash was forthcoming to keep me up a third year. I hoped against hope that I could stay on. I was enjoying myself enormously and of all colleges, Magdalen was, to my mind, easily the most beautiful and satisfying.
There wasn't a moment that I didn't grasp and love.

After my first term I was allotted rooms in college, rather dark rooms in cloisters. They had the advantage of looking across a sward of perfectly kept turf to the New Buildings. An artist friend of mine once described them as the most beautiful buildings in Oxford.

They possessed another advantage. They enabled me to get a little surreptitious practice at golf. I was never more than a duffer at the game, but the thought that the taking of such licence with their beautiful turf might not meet with the entire approval of the Fellows lent a certain spice to the proceedings. I had bought, in a local sports shop, a captive golf ball. Fastened to the ball was a length of elastic and cord. Having tee'd up and driven off, the ball was brought to a gradual halt by the combined pull of its various attachments. On one occasion I saw a don approaching from the New Buildings. This, I thought, would be the end of my harmless little game. Luckily I remembered that he himself was a keen golfer. As he drew near I asked him to come and try his hand at it. I was somewhat surprised when he fell in with my suggestion and with obvious enjoyment drove off three or four times before he went on his way. It was never suggested that my driving practice was not in the best interests of the turf and nothing untoward occurred, though I had one moment of anxiety when the elastic parted half way up its length and the ball went sailing comet-like towards Addison's Walk. In the ordinary course of events it would have proved the drive of a lifetime.

Those of us who went up to Oxford as freshmen after the war never realized what an emotional strain it was for many of those who had been up prior to 1914 and had returned to complete their studies after the war. Despite the fact that they soon made many lasting friendships with a younger generation that had only recently come into residence, there was no doubt that the thought of all their pre-war contemporaries who would never come back drove them on occasions into extravagances completely foreign to their character. For them there were too many ghosts of former friends, too vividly remembered.

There was one such on whom we were relying to complete

"SHIP MONEY, YOU BLOODY FOOL!"

our college eight, which was going for the Grand Challenge Cup at Henley. One evening we were playing bridge in a suite of rooms overlooking the River Cherwell (which had been occupied by Oscar Wilde when he was up at Magdalen). Suddenly this dear man took up a bottle of whisky and putting it to his mouth proceeded to pour it down his throat. He must have consumed nearly half a bottle at one gulp. In a short time he was completely unconscious. Our one fear was that this lapse would be discovered by the authorities, in which case it would be long odds against them allowing him to row for the college at Henley. Careful watch was kept on him. He wasn't living in college, so a bed was rigged up for him on the spot. The next day he was still unconscious, and when by evening he had shown no signs of coming to, it was obvious that something had to be done. It so happened that there was an old rowing blue who had been up at Magdalen some thirty years before, who was now a doctor practising in Oxford. He was only too willing to help. He was smuggled into college, and as he arrived at the bedside the patient opened his eyes for the first time in twenty-four hours and murmured, "I say, you chaps, you needn't bother to wait up for me." It never occurred to him — why should it? — that several friends had been, in fact, "waiting up" for him for some considerable time. However, the application of a stomach pump worked wonders and by the next day he was completely recovered.

During my second year, beyond attending lectures regularly and showing up my weekly essay, I am ashamed to say that I did very little work. My way was paved with good intentions. I took away a number of books to read during Boat Race training. I even went so far as to cart a weighty caseful of volumes out to the South of France. Needless to say, other attractions won the day and I failed to open one of them.

Quite suddenly I realized that I should fail to obtain a degree unless I took some rather drastic steps. I concluded the best thing would be to study past history papers and train myself to write a reasonable response to every question. I argued that on any one period of history only certain questions could be asked. I realized they wouldn't be phrased in the same way, but with a few deft introductory remarks I reckoned I should be able to twist the question so that it accorded with one on which I had worked previously. It was my last term. We regained the Headship of the River, which we had lost some two years previously. Practice for this event occupied most of the afternoon. To make up for this time I worked far into the night, until I was so tired that the lines I was reading started running into each other while individual words indulged in strange gyrations on the page.

The dread day arrived. On my first sight of each paper I had the feeling that I couldn't answer a single question. How well I remember the asides and injunctions accompanying each paper. "Write on one side of the paper only." "The answering of questions two, five and seven is compulsory." What a nightmare! When the ordeal was finished I felt I had done myself less than justice.

After the lapse of a week or more, I was invited to attend for my Viva Voce. Here was at least one consolation. Whatever your replies, you could only improve your chances. It was always said that Vivas were invariably centred around your weakest subject. If this was a fact, mine was Modern History. "To what single factor do you attribute the Civil War?" My mind raced round in small circles without picking up a clue. With very little chance of success I tried to bluff. "Personally I have a feeling that the King's journey north to plead with the Scottish bishops made the Civil War a certainty." "Wasn't there anything else?" they asked. "There were a number of things," I said. "But I've always felt that that ill-advised visit was the last straw."

It was over a year later, lying in bed early one morning in my parents' house without a thought of scholastic matters, that the answer suddenly filtered through. I murmured to myself "Ship money, you bloody fool! Ship money!"

In due course the results were published. I had got a Fourth. Would Ship Money have given me a Third? Was a Fourth an act of charity, awarded out of the kindness of their hearts? I shall never know. I don't think they award Fourths

"SHIP MONEY, YOU BLOODY FOOL!"

now. Whenever, somewhat reluctantly, I have to admit to a humble Fourth, invariably I follow it up by adding, "Of course it's a far greater distinction than getting a First. Don't forget there are more Firsts awarded than Fourths."

I went down from Magdalen with a heavy heart. I had enjoyed every moment. It is true that I would dearly have loved to have shone scholastically, in addition to a certain accomplishment which I had shown on the river. However, as I had hoped, the outstanding thing that Oxford had done for me was to rid me of my ghastly inferiority complex.

People have said many unkind things about Warren. They accused him of being a snob. I held him in great affection. When at last I had taken leave of Magdalen (and I do hope that this does not sound terribly egotistical and smug), he wrote to my mother—"Dear Mrs. Nickalls, Some three years ago you wrote and assured me that should I take Oliver into Magdalen I would never regret it. I am bound to admit that you were absolutely right...." That he should have remembered it, I find astonishing; that he should have taken the trouble to write it, I find particularly touching.

Chapter 10

Across The Herring Pond

Soon after the Henley Regatta of 1923 I received an invitation to row in a Leander crew in a regatta to be staged as an adjunct to the Canadian National Exhibition in Toronto. I was just about to accept when, much to my surprise, I received a letter from my father which dampened my spirits a good deal. He had heard that I had received an invitation to row in Canada. He hoped most sincerely that I would refuse. He was against international competition. The definition of an amateur abroad did not coincide with our own understanding of the term, and had in the past proved most unsatisfactory; on occasions it had engendered a good deal of bitter feeling.

To say that I was surprised would be an under-statement. I was amazed. Was it the possible expense? Leander were looking after that, nor did I think that the fifteen or twenty pounds for my out-of-pocket expenses, which he would be called upon to provide, would have caused him to write as he did. Nevertheless I felt that head-on confrontation on the subject might have led to a rift between us—a rift I was anxious to avoid. Fortunately C. M. Pitman, an old Oxford blue, was going with the crew as coach. I wrote to him and explained my predicament; and a few days later, in a casual sort of way, my father announced that he had changed his mind and that I could go to Toronto if I wanted to.

Towards the end of August we set sail on the maiden voyage of *S.S. Doric*. We were a party of fourteen—the crew, plus the cox and spare man and the Cambridge University boatman, "Cooey" Philipps. "Cherry" Pitman, his name was Charles, but "Cherry" he had always been since his university days, brought along his wife. The first morning out a heavy sea was running. Dutifully we rose early and indulged in our usual pre-breakfast run round and round the main deck. This was not a particularly easy accomplishment in a rolling ship. One moment we were toiling up an exhausting incline, the next we were hurtling down a steep slope virtually out of control. There were several complaints from those who, in the throes of sea-sickness, were occupying the cabins immediately below our route. Quite naturally, in their delicate condition, they didn't relish the din of what must have sounded like a herd of elephants trampling overhead. We saw their point and postponed our activities to a more reasonable hour.

Eventually we docked at Quebec, some thirty-six hours behind schedule. We were informed that the Speaker of the Canadian Parliament was there to meet us. We made our way to the rails and peered down at the dockside. "Those two there," announced someone at my elbow. "The older one is the Speaker — Joe Knight, and the other is Ernie Laidlaw." It appeared that these two were the sole survivors of a reception committee which had travelled from Toronto to Montreal to give us a welcoming dinner party the previous evening. Our non-arrival was not allowed to interfere with their party, which took place whilst we were still at sea. In spite of our absence we were delighted to learn that it had been a great success. They had obviously enjoyed "one hell of an evening" and dined, not wisely but too well. In the event the two on the quayside were the only ones who felt in a fit state to continue the journey from Montreal to Quebec. The remainder, we gathered, were sleeping off the effects of the dinner in honour of our non-arrival.

I must admit that the appearance of the Speaker from Ontario, Joe Knight, came as something of a surprise — a thickset rotund man in a flamboyant check suit, and a straw hat with a colourful hatband, worn at a jaunty angle. His hair was white and his face purple. From one pocket there hung some mustard-coloured silk pyjamas. From the other pocket peeped what appeared to be the stopper and neck of a bottle of gin. After what he had been through in the previous forty-eight hours it should have been obvious to us that he stood in some need of an occasional stimulant. Within a few minutes he was on deck and we soon found that his somewhat racy exterior enclosed a heart of gold. "I'm Joe Knight," he announced. "But call me Knightee. What's your name?" he asked our coach. "Pitman," came the reply. Slapping him on the back, he cried, "Pit, old man, looks as though you've got a swell lot of boys here." He turned to me, "What's your name?" "Nickalls," I told him. "Nick, old boy, it's grand to meet you. You come from Oxford or Cambridge?" As soon as it became obvious that each one of us would be known by the first syllable of our name, we rushed to see what misunderstandings would follow from other introductions.

Knightee stayed on board and continued the voyage from Quebec to Montreal in our company. He was a host in himself, and aided and abetted by Ernie Laidlaw did a miraculously fine piece of Public Relations work. On arrival at Montreal, not a moment was lost. We were to catch the midnight train on to Toronto. Our party was then divided; Cherry and Mrs. Cherry with one or two of the more staid members of the party were entertained by Knightee, whilst the rest of us were handed over to Ernie. We were driven at a furious pace round Montreal, and paid a hurried visit to McGill University—far too hurried to get any very comprehensive impression of the place. We were taken into the chapel, where it was pointed out that they had fashioned some stained-glass windows from splinters and pieces of broken stained glass that their military had picked up from the ruins of various cathedrals and churches in Flanders.

I envied them their splendidly equipped theatre, something far more complete and sophisticated than could be found at Oxford or Cambridge. Did they think their playhouse was perhaps lacking in tradition or historical associations? This deficiency they were determined to make good. They had erected a number of glass cases in which they displayed various theatrical trivia. Amongst this collection I noticed a pair of long, white kid gloves which, as their label announced, had been used by no less an actress than Marie Lohr when she had appeared there.

ACROSS THE HERRING POND

I would dearly have loved to have seen more of the University, but our kind guide had other things in store. We were ordered back into our cars, driven to another part of the town, and after some door-knocking and bell-ringing were ushered into a dreary looking establishment, where we were shown into a large empty room and invited to take our seats on a row of gilt chairs. There was a piano but precious little else. What on earth was this all about? We were not kept long in suspense. A bevy of semi-clad harridans filed into the room. Could Canadian hospitality go further? They had even gone so far as to put a brothel at our disposal, presumably at no extra charge. We goggled as the troupe filed in and took up positions facing us. We were in training, and any form of sexual activity was taboo. Nowadays there would be, no doubt, plenty of people willing to declare that sexual activity was far preferable to sexual frustration. In this case, however, there was no frustration. The ladies of that particular establishment being, to say the least of it, distinctly unappetizing. Anyhow, the goggling had to stop. One of the troupe broke the silence: "Come on, boys. What's wrong with you? Are you shy or something?" One of our number, more conversant with brothel junketings than the rest, spoke up. "Why don't you do something? Sing, dance, play the piano. Put on a show!" An invitation to which there was no response. So far as we were concerned the confrontation was at an end. As one man we rose and made for the door. An angry buzz of dissatisfaction came from the troupe. Quite naturally they inferred that their charms were insufficient to excite our attentions. Our pace quickened as their fury rose; only to be assuaged by the piles of notes our guide pressed into the avaricious hands of the Madame. It was with a certain sense of relief that we heard the front door close behind us.

We then rejoined the rest of our party and boarded the night train for Toronto. As we cleared our luggage the next morning, Joe Knight persuaded our cox to carry a heavy bag for him through the Customs. When we arrived at our headquarters, the Edward VII Hotel, the bag was taken straight up to a bedroom. No one was surprised when it was found to contain several bottles of gin. Prohibition reigned in the State of Ontario at that time, and Joe Knight's political party, whichever it was, had—so I was told—come to power on the prohibition ticket. A minor detail such as *that* wasn't going to stand in the way of Joe's thirst. As one of his buddies said to me, "You know, Mrs. Knight thinks I encourage Joe to go on the booze. With her I'm just about as popular as a skunk at a garden party." It was eight o'clock in the morning when, in the privacy of a bedroom, the first bottle was opened. As we passed the door we could hear Joe addressing our cox 'Jock' Clapperton. "Old boy, you must always put the empties into the wastepaper basket. If you find it's full, put them out into the passage, but outside somebody else's door."

It was not long before we were asked to reassemble on the steps of the hotel. A bevy of photographers and reporters awaited us. Joe, suitably refreshed, descended from a bedroom. As soon as he appeared one of the reporters called out to him, "Joe, you old devil, you've been bringing liquor into the State again." "Cross my heart, man, I've never brought a drop of liquor into this State." Technically, this may have been true, providing he had been fortunate in persuading somebody to carry it for him.

As we posed for the cameras, questions were fired at us from every direction, and every detail of our lives was faithfully recorded by the local press. "Their Captain, the Reverend Humphrey Playford, was ordained in the Ministry last year. David Raikes, their number four, comes from one of the foremost military families in Britain." As he and his four brothers had collected something like seven D.S.O.s and six M.C.s between them in the First World War, this statement was perhaps not so wide of the mark as it first appeared.

At this juncture we were introduced to a remarkable character—Tommy Church. I cannot remember whether he was actually Mayor of Toronto at the time, but he left us in no doubt that he had been. "Hi yer—I'm Tommy Church. Call me Tommy. I've been Mayor of this city seven times. In the whole history of Toronto no one's been

Mayor as many times as I have. Over there we have a brand-new custom house. Last year this city took (and he mentioned the figure) million dollars in customs." It was through a series of similarly explosive and random utterances that we got to know and love this astonishing character during the next week or so. His sheer enthusiasm for the mother country was touching in its sincerity. Later that morning he escorted us down to the lakeside, where we boarded a launch to go up to our allotted boathouse. Tommy never drew breath. His conversation was studded with *non sequiturs*. "What I say is — the British Fleet is the best League of Nations. That's a damn fat seagull." The connection between the two was never revealed.

It was that first morning we discovered that our rowing took place behind a string of breakwaters running parallel with the shore some two or three hundred yards out. Outside this line of breakwaters the water was too rough for serious rowing. The line of breakwaters was not continuous. At intervals there were gaps through which rough water lumbered up on to the shore. These gaps had to be negotiated with some caution. We found this out on our very first outing. A goodly crowd had assembled by the time we pushed off from the raft. We had taken only half a dozen strokes when we struck a vicious wave and came to a halt, narrowly missing capsizing. This taught us a salutory lesson, and from then on our cox kept his eyes open for similar rough water hazards.

I will not go into details of our progress as a crew. But for the record I will mention that there were four entries for the eight-oared event. In the first two heats the Undine Barge Club, American champions of that year, beat the Argonauts of Toronto Boat Club, whilst we triumphed over Toronto University. In the final we beat the Undines with something to spare.

The Canadian authorities were kind enough to present us with a handsome silver trophy. This was not for winning our event but rather for making the journey to compete. So insistent were they that we should have something tangible to bring home that they made the presentation some days

A RAINBOW IN THE SKY

before the Regatta, which we felt was most considerate of them. In presenting their cup, Tommy Church, I think it was, made the following remark to the assembled company. "D'you realize, you fellas, that the parents of these boys are being taxed out of existence to provide us with the finest fleet in the world?" Beside this flag-waving utterance our own particular brand of patriotism was made to appear a very lukewarm affair.

During the whole of our stay we scanned the Canadian papers every day. The particular style of journalism employed to record our doings was vivid, racy and a constant source of delight. The water of Lake Ontario was in rowing parlance "lively". This indicates to oarsmen a good depth of water which gives an added buoyancy and complete lack of the "drag" that one so often experiences in this country. We attributed the near disaster of our initial outing to the "lively" water. This gave birth to the following: "As a matter of fact the water is a bit too lively for them," as Major David Raikes remarked. "That water sure is lively but my, how we did fly when we hit up our racing pace." There was no one less likely to have used this particular phraseology than David Raikes. In the same article "Members of the English party are apt to refer to their crew as a 'pick-up' crew. Pick-up? Not by the length of an Irish Uncle. Hand-picked and one swell crew." "Not by the length of an Irish uncle." Neither before nor since have I ever heard the expression nor can I imagine how it originated.

In those far-off days the neighbouring township of Hamilton, situated like Toronto on the shores of Lake Ontario, was known, as I believe it is to this day, as "the ambitious city". This gave rise to the following caption. "Ambitious city plans to send crew to C.N.E. (Canadian National Exhibition) Regatta." A curious headline to those unacquainted with local rivalries.

At that time one of the requirements of amateur oarsmen in this country was that, while in the boat, they should be clothed from the knee to the elbow. This get-up contrasted strangely with the singlet and briefs sported by our rivals —

a contrast that did not go unnoticed. One report pointed out that the "Leander chappies" wore shorts and zephyrs with short sleeves and "By comparison their Argonaut pals look like so many debutantes at a Cuban Ball". When we rowed our first course "Cherry" Pitman was reported as saying, "I told them before they rowed that I wouldn't speak to any one of them who didn't row himself right out. I shall speak to them all tonight," smiled the imperturbable British rowing expert. As the day of the race approached we were informed that "Leander's superiority stands out like gumboils on an elephant". And then describing our eventual victory, it recorded that after half way our cox kept on having to glance over his shoulder to keep in touch with the enemy. It continued, "Leander's winning effort was like a ballet on water. Not the sort of ballet which stresses the random waving of arms and legs, but the neo-classical ballet where leg work is all important."

Our Canadian visit was coming to an end. I have always been grateful to our hosts for all the trouble they took to make our stay a particularly happy one. A Sunday trip across to Niagara, dinner at the Hunt Club, and a thousand and one little kindnesses which made our trip quite unforgettable. Now, through the generosity of Robert F. Herrick we were to be given the chance of a week or so in the States.

Bob Herrick — a doyen amongst American rowing men — was a great favourite at Henley Regatta. Being a man of means he had on various occasions brought crews of the Boston Union Boat Club to compete at the Regatta. He was kind enough to ask us to stay at his expense at the Harvard Club in Boston. Whilst there Frank Peabody, who was well known to previous generations of oarsmen in this country, did all he could for us. At that time he was a comparatively old man, which did not deter him from driving us here, there and everywhere at what seemed a furious and dangerous pace for one so advanced in years. He and his wife were accustomed to make regular trips to England. Their interests, however, lay in different directions. He was a keen follower of the turf, while she showed a strong preference for cathedrals. Both followed their natural bent; a perfectly amicable arrangement which kept them happy and perforce apart.

Frank took some of us out to the Myopic Club one day. It seemed a strange name until he explained that it had been founded by a body of men, all of whom happened to be short-sighted. We learned from him that, later in the week, a clambake had been arranged in our honour, and that we would be driven out some sixty miles from Boston to where a long, sandy beach provided a suitable venue.

I must say that for sheer entertainment it proved something to be remembered. It was my first clambake, and now at an interval of fifty years it seems likely to prove my last. It was a cloudless day. We arrived just before lunch and our attention was drawn immediately to what looked like a number of miniature, smoking bonfires which lined the beach. We were invited to take a plate and probe what, on closer inspection, proved to be small heaps of steaming seaweed. By raking the seaweed around we discovered a delicious assortment of seafood — clams, crabs and lobsters — all ready cooked. We piled a selection on to our plates and, despite Prohibition, armed ourselves with a goblet of rum punch and repaired to enjoy our plunder. Meanwhile a Cuban band played a selection of their more riotous numbers. "You know why we Americans shout so much?" screamed an old dame into my ear. "It's because all our lives we have to shout down those goddamn bands. It's sheer hell!"

We ate and drank. The sun was overpowering and that "goddamn" band never let up. Some of the party, armed with bottles, got in a dinghy and rowed out to a motor cruiser anchored offshore. Others, in spite of the blaring trumpets, snatched a few winks of sleep on the beach. At last the band, like ourselves, took a rest, and the party relapsed into a well-earned siesta. Peace reigned. Nothing stirred for about forty-five minutes. The occupants of the motor cruiser were the first to show signs of life. They clambered up on to the deck and started throwing each other into the sea. This was the signal for the orchestra to break once more into a ragtime medley.

ACROSS THE HERRING POND

Meanwhile on shore many of the party were preparing for a bathe. Much to our surprise Mrs. "Cherry" appeared from nowhere in an elaborately modelled swim suit, highly decorative and most discreet. Not an inch of skin was showing. Bikinis were as yet unknown. Her appearance was the signal for a white-haired old man to come running to her side. He doffed his straw hat, bowed and offered his hand. She took it and was escorted to the water's edge. Pretending to be overcome by her sheer beauty, he waded straight into the sea, fully clothed, until only his head and straw hat were above the water. Could gallantry go further? This episode came as a fitting climax to a wonderful day.

At the end of the week thanks again to Bob Herrick, our party moved down to New York. We arrived there in the evening and awaited our first chance of exploring the city in daylight with keen anticipation. I regret now that I never visited Haarlem. A newly wed cousin of mine took his bride there for an evening's entertainment. Sitting at an adjacent table was a lone negro of gigantic proportions. As my cousin, a good-looking, slightly-built man, took his seat he was warned, "Mind your step with that negro at the next table. Agree to whatever he suggests. When aroused or thwarted in any way he's extremely dangerous." The band struck up. A few couples started dancing. Much to his horror, my cousin noticed the dark giant of whom he had been forewarned advancing towards his table. "Say, buddy, will you dance?" asked the negro. "Yes," gasped my cousin, whereupon he was grasped round the waist and was forced to one-step round the room at a furious pace. The band stopped and he was returned ignominiously to his wife. "Thank God that's over," he murmured. But it wasn't. The band embarked on a new number. Back stalked the negro. "Care to dance again?" Again his victim had not the courage to refuse. "Yes." Round and round he was whirled in a frenzy of dancing. The negro was ecstatic. Beaming down into his partner's face, he whispered, "Say, Buddy, I've fallen for you in a big way." "Yes?" came the horror-stricken reply, and as the band stopped he was returned again to his wife. "That's a fine way to behave on your honeymoon," she complained. "You bring me to Haarlem and then you dance with a damn negro all night."

But to return to my stay in New York; after a week our party, with the exception of David Raikes and myself, sailed for home. He had engaged some sort of sleeping accommodation and intended to stay on for another ten days. He asked me if I would care to keep him company. I jumped at the chance. This accommodation, we discovered, was fairly primitive—one room with twin beds and adjoining bathroom. There were blankets, sheets and pillowcases, but not one single stick of furniture, not even a wardrobe or chest of drawers. We lived in our suitcases. Moreover the whole apartment was covered in thick layers of dust. It cannot have been cleaned for years. To get from the bathroom to our beds we had to lay down a gangway of newspapers to prevent our feet from collecting a coating of filth before we got between the sheets. We paid a Japanese, whom we never actually met, to come in and tidy up. I cannot remember that we paid anything for the room. Looking back on it, I suppose we were very lucky to find anything at all. For breakfast we found a cafe just down the street, patronized by truck drivers and other tough customers, where you could get quite a good meal for half a dollar.

Speculation was rife at this time as regards the outcome of the World's Heavyweight Boxing Championship which was being staged at Madison Square Garden that very week between the reigning champion, Jack Dempsey and Louis Firpo.

Those two names were far too ordinary for the press boys. Something far more exciting, colourful and descriptive had to be found. In inch-high headlines we were asked to speculate as to the chances of the Wild Bull of the Pampas putting paid to the Manassa Mauler. I had not as yet learned which pseudonym applied to which.

As it was probably the only time in my life I should get a chance of seeing a heavyweight world title fight, we went down to the Garden and bought our tickets, the dollar equivalent of £3 each. We armed ourselves with field

ACROSS THE HERRING POND

glasses and arriving in good time were delighted to find that we were not half as far from the ringside as I had feared.

After the usual preliminaries, the bout started. We did not have to wait for long for the fireworks. A vicious right hook, a blow that would have felled an ox, flashed on to Firpo's chin and down he went. As soon as he got to his feet Dempsey returned to the attack — sometimes to the head, sometimes to the body. His punishing body blows I remember in particular. Often it seemed that his fists had to carry but a bare eighteen inches to find their mark. On many such occasions he seemed able to judge to a nicety the damage he had done for, having delivered them, he would stand back and watch Firpo as with buckling knees he tottered drunkenly to the canvas.

Suddenly, having picked himself up no less than seven times Firpo seemed to realize that desperate measures were called for, so summoning all his remaining strength he unleashed a vicious two-fisted attack on Dempsey's head and torso. Not a quick tattoo of blows but a deliberate left-right, left-right, almost as though one were watching it in slow motion; half punches, half pushes. This unexpected assault had Dempsey on the retreat; back he went right through the ropes, bang on to the typewriter of an unsuspecting journalist busy on ringside reporting.

There was a hushed pause and Dempsey climbed back into the ring. My own feeling was that he was more surprised than shaken. Only once before in his whole glorious career had he been off his feet, far less through the ropes. Once more in the ring he took a few quick steps along the ropes, sliding his gloved hand along the topmost rope as he did so.

Could Firpo mount another herculean attack? Whether or no is immaterial. The fact remains — he didn't. Had Dempsey ever been on the hook which I doubt, a second or so's respite and he was after his opponent again when the bell signalled the end of that first astonishing and incident-packed round.

From the opening of the second round, a confident Dempsey had the measure of his opponent. He waded in and knocked him down. For the eighth time a weary Firpo rose from the canvas only to be knocked down and counted out. A short fight, but so spellbinding and exciting that at a distance of fifty years I seem to remember it blow by blow.

Curiously enough I don't remember the roar of the crowd. Did the pace and ferocity of the proceedings stun them into comparative silence? This may well have been the case, because I distinctly remember the sound of gloves pounding on bare flesh was distinctly audible. Somehow it conjured up a curious impression of two prehistoric giants belabouring each other with clubs.

Time was running out. We enjoyed two or three happy weekends with friends on Long Island — one of these was with Ashley Sparks and his charming family. He ran the Cunard-White Star empire in America and it was he who provided us with a luxurious homeward passage on the *Aquitania*.

Chapter 11

Unemployed! Unemployable?

ON my return home the first item on my agenda was to find myself a job. Looking back I find it absolutely astounding that I could have been so casual about this, for me, all-important matter. I had made no plans nor had I taken even tentative soundings as to how I might support myself. Did this argue a most colossal conceit on my part? Did I fondly imagine that, out of the blue, someone would offer me some important, lucrative position, or did I think that one of my or my father's friends would point to a desk and issue an invitation for me to join their firm? Why the hell should they? Such thoughts didn't enter my head. The fact was I had been far too busy enjoying myself to give it more than a fleeting thought.

I had always had an urge to make the stage my career. Ever since my mother, some twenty years before, had urged me to "establish the pigtail" I had flirted with the idea. I had played time and again in amateur theatricals — not entirely unsuccessfully, and had devised, directed and played in a number of revues which we put on every year at Farnham Royal. During the past few years I had struck up a firm friendship with John Drinkwater. We had met originally through his cousin George, a dear man who had rowed for Oxford some twenty years previously and was at that time rowing correspondent for the *Daily Telegraph*. "Cousin John" as we called him took me to lunch at the Garrick and was kind enough to offer me a walking-on part in *Robert Burns* — a play he was planning to stage in the near future. At the same time he gave me an introduction to Robert Lorraine, who at that time was playing in a Restoration comedy at the Lyric, Hammersmith. I kept an appointment to meet him there in his dressing-room. As soon as he learned the object of my visit, he simply couldn't wait to get rid of me. He was frank and quite ruthless. "After all, you haven't got much to offer," he commented. "But I tell you what I'll do. I'll give you a letter of introduction to a film-making friend of mine. You'll probably find him in New York, but if you miss him there you're sure to catch up with him in Hollywood." How he thought that I, with no more than ten pounds to my name, was going to get to New York, far less to Hollywood, he never said. The whole idea seemed ludicrously problematical, if not farcical—the wildest, wild-goose chase imaginable. I thanked him profusely, and as he had made no suggestion that I should sit out in front to see the last two acts of his play, I staggered forth into the night.

My father, meanwhile, had been extraordinarily forbearing. He had, he said, no wish to stand in my way, were I bent on a theatrical career. He warned me that the going would be tough. He had consulted an old friend of his, one Bromley Davenport, who confessed that though for the last thirty years his name had shone in electric lights outside numerous London theatres, he had never made enough money on which to marry.

I thought it over carefully. I wanted to continue my rowing career whilst health and strength were still on my side. I realized too that, at heart, I was a lover of routine. As the sporting and social calendar rotated, I loved doing the same sort of things at the same time year after year. Added to this I was acutely aware that I was burdened with a most unprepossessing face which, except for the thug parts, would prove an almost insurmountable handicap through the years. By chance I learned that Eddie Russell, my junior by a year or so, had become a cub reporter on the *Daily Express*, so persuading myself that I had no wish to cram a bowler on to my head and catch the same train to the same office day after day I presented myself to the Editor of the *Express*. I was engaged on the understanding that I should be paid the princely sum of fourpence a line for anything of

UNEMPLOYED! UNEMPLOYABLE?

mine they might publish until such time as I should have established myself.

That, as I soon found out, led to a variety of assignations. On my first morning I was told to go out and report on a demonstration of a new type of humane killer in north London. There was quite a party of us by the time I arrived. We were then conducted to a slaughter house where an unwilling cow with a rope round its neck was dragged in, a revolver-like instrument put against its forehead, and the trigger pulled. The collapse of the cow was followed by the inevitable grisly details; all part and parcel of animal slaughter. On my return to Fleet Street I wrote my piece. This was not as easy as it may sound. Never having been in a slaughter house before, I had nothing with which to compare this new type of killer. However I concocted what I felt to be a fair description of the proceedings and handed it in. Five minutes later the Editor advanced to where I was sitting in the News Room. "Look here, Nickalls," he said. "This is all very well for a Leader in *The Times* but it's no damn good for our paper. Did you see any pigs slaughtered? You did? Did they squeal?" "No, they didn't," I replied. "You'll see I have written there 'death was instantaneous' in which case they couldn't have squealed." "Our readers don't know what instantaneous means," he shouted. It was useless to argue. The following morning this headline appeared "Pigs did not Squeal".

The next day I was called into an inner office. My attention was drawn to the announcement of a wedding which had taken place at a Registry Office. There was reason to believe that one of the parties was already married. The possibility of bigamy was mooted, but first they required proof that this report of the Registry Office wedding was correct. Would I go and buy, from the Registrar, a copy of the vital document. I hustled off to the address given to be greeted by a delightful, silver-haired, mild-mannered old man. As he copied out the certificate, he remarked how curious it was that people should be sufficiently interested to require such a document. I had no idea whether, were bigamy to have been proved, he would have got into trouble. I only know that his bland, friendly manner made me feel an absolute brute. Years after these events, I was discussing some of my experiences with that incomparable wit, J. B. Morton — Beachcomber of the *Daily Express*. It appears that he too, when he started in Fleet Street, had been sent down to interview a poor woman who had suffered a particularly agonizing bereavement. On his return to the office an editor avid for some sort of sensationalism asked him, "Tell me, did you get her grief? DID YOU GET HER GRIEF?" Whereupon he vowed he would have nothing more to do with such beastliness and turned to writing his humorous column, with which he has been adding to the gaiety of the public for over half a century.

My job the next morning was to go to Selfridges where they were presenting prizes to the winners of a knitting competition. Nothing very news-worthy about that, except that a male knitter had won third prize. The presentation was over when I arrived but I traced this phenomenon to the restaurant where I found a particularly colourless young man munching a very dull-looking piece of fried plaice, and I got his story. In the afternoon I went to a matinee and watched a pair of Russian dancers — the Zaharoffs, a husband and wife partnership who displayed a rather unexciting routine. On returning home that evening my younger brother asked me what my day had been. I told him — "You seem to have had an enthralling day," he remarked. "I would gladly have paid to do what you've been paid to do."

My most riveting experience came the next day. Landon Ronald had just announced that he intended to employ only British artistes at his forthcoming concerts. Would I go and obtain the reactions of none other than the famous contralto, Marguerite d'Alvarez, to this publicity seeking announcement? One story had been told me about this colourful personality, a story which had come through the wife of George Drinkwater, who had married a dear woman who sang quite beautifully under the name of Carmen Hill. It appears that at a rather stuffy tea party, d'Alvarez had remarked, "You know when I first came to this country

UNEMPLOYED! UNEMPLOYABLE?

everyone said that I was Reinhardt's mistress." This gave reign to a spate of comments. "Of course not, darling." "What a beastly thing to say!" "How unkind can some people be." "But I was!" d'Alvarez exclaimed.

I think I interviewed her in her suite at the Savoy. She had been having some flashlight photos taken and she wanted me to know it. She came into the room backwards, fanning away the remains of the flashlight smoke with a newspaper as she made this somewhat unconventional entrance. "All this beastly smoke — I'm so sorry," she said as she shook my hand. I asked her opinion of Landon Ronald's announcement. Without a second's hesitation she followed up my cue and launched herself into the following dramatic pronouncement. "Musicians are but messengers of beauty, birds of passage. We artistes have no country and need no passports." This was great stuff. I sat spellbound. As a little encouragement I mentioned America. "Ah," and she wagged an admonitory finger in my direction. "I'm not going to make any bad blood between you and the Americans. They are a young, virile race. I am the only artiste in my family. They are all Service and Diplomatic people and like you English, they are frightened. All frightened! Frightened of what, I should like to know; the unexpected? Only the other day a girl wrote to me and said that that thing I sing 'God shall wipe away all tears' was the only thing that had prevented her from committing suicide. I have possibly ten more years of concert work before me. If in that time I can bring this beauty, this happiness to the humblest of God's creatures, I shall be satisfied. Goodbye, Mr. Nickalls, and perhaps one day ... somewhere ... somehow we shall meet again. Who knows?" The interview was at an end. It had exceeded my wildest expectations. Next morning on the front page there ran the perfect caption "Messengers of beauty. Birds of passage." The most rewarding interview I had ever experienced. At the end of a week or so, I realized that, though quite a bit of my copy had seen the light of day, I wasn't going to make a living wage at fourpence a line, unless I could turn in and get printed at least twenty or thirty times as much. That simply wasn't on, and I concluded that unless the *Express* was willing to employ me on some less chancy basis I was wasting my time. There were others in my position, making a pittance and too afraid to ask for more for fear they would get the push. I thought I'd take a chance. I asked to see the Editor, telling him in advance the object of the interview. As soon as I arrived in his sanctum he began, "I've made enquiries and they don't seem to think you're going to make much of a journalist, Nickalls. I don't really know what you could do. I suppose you could become a half-commission man on the Stock Exchange." This riled me a good deal, and I wasn't going to be patronized. "You needn't worry on my behalf," I said, implying at the same time that the proprietor of the *Daily Express* was the only one who need worry. "I've only to walk out into the street and there are plenty of people jostling each other for my services," I assured him. What bravado! And what a damnable lie. No one wanted me, and as far as I could see no one would ever want me. I shook hands and swept out. I have read the *Daily Express* regularly ever since.

I returned home and was thankful that I had at least a roof over my head. I had no regular allowance and had to go to my father for every penny. After all the money he had spent on my education it must have come as something of a shock to find that he had to continue to keep me. I was unemployable. Every now and then I heard of a possible opening, and would journey to London in search of a job; all to no purpose. An idea was forming in my mind that I might enter advertising on the creative side. Somehow I sensed that the whole subject was in its infancy and would develop and expand enormously in the years to come. My father at this time was employed by an advertising agency by the name of Walter Judd, and was doing what he could to bring business their way. I had no right to think they would employ me, and anyhow they specialized in financial advertising and that was not really a branch of the business in which I felt that whatever creative ability I might possess would be given any real scope. Life in fact was pretty grim and I don't think I have ever felt so helpless and so utterly miserable. Should I ever get going? After nearly five

UNEMPLOYED! UNEMPLOYABLE?

months of frustration and idleness there came a gleam of hope. The Magdalen College eight of the previous summer had been stroked by a very promising youngster by the name of Gifford Fox. His father, Sir Gilbert Fox, had made his own way in life, working his way to a position of great prominence on the sugar market in Liverpool. Gifford was kind enough to ask if I would care to go up to Liverpool where his father would do his best to get me a job. This kind gesture was made all the more attractive when I learned that my visit would coincide with a house-party the Fox's were giving in connection with the Grand National. I grasped the opportunity, packed my bags and caught a train to Liverpool. They gave me a marvellous week, dinner parties, balls or some other entertainment every night, whilst the racing was viewed from the Fox's box where sumptuous luncheons were served every day.

This was absolute heaven after the somewhat drab life I had been leading and I can never thank that family sufficiently for the great kindness and generosity they showed me. It was unforgettable. Nor amongst all the festivities did the question of my future go unattended. Waiting until one of his guests had wined and dined and was therefore possibly at his most vulnerable, Gilbert Fox would edge him into a corner and tell him point-blank that the least he could do would be to give me a job. In fact I caught him in the act on at least two occasions. I have never ceased to have the most affectionate memories of that dear man. Sometimes I think his kindliness sprang from a certain fellow feeling when he looked back and recalled his own early struggles. He died a millionaire and confided to me that at the age of thirty his salary was no more than three hundred a year.

The last day of my visit arrived and Gilbert Fox suggested that Gifford should take me over to see Lord Leverhulme. I was rather nervous at the prospect of this interview. I needn't have been, for it never took place. Lord Leverhulme wouldn't be back until late that evening. I remember strolling round his garden. What a taskmaster he must have been! Not a single weed was to be found there. It was as if the gardeners had just been at work on it and, having detected our presence, had scurried off into the undergrowth until we had passed.

However, that visit was very far from fruitless. Within a fortnight I had received a letter from William Lever (who eventually succeeded his father the first Viscount) asking me to go and see him at the Lever Brothers Headquarters hard by Blackfriars Bridge. The interview was short and, as far as I was concerned, particularly sweet. He engaged me, and on his giving me the choice of what department I would enter I opted for the advertising department. I would be paid £250 a year and I could start the following week. Oh my God, what a relief! At last I had landed a job.

The copywriting department to which I was accredited consisted of some six individuals, and when a request came through for a piece of copy for a certain product, each one of us had a shot at it and one of our efforts was eventually selected. This outfit was presided over by a rather cosy man by the name of Clennel Wilkinson. He briefed us, gave us the number of words required. As a sideline he wrote books and his biography of Lord Nelson was received by the critics with much approbation. He was a friendly, easy-going man, very fond of his mid-day tipple and inclined to become somnolent after lunch. He felt it was his duty to inspire us to give of our best. Some copy was required for jellies with various fruit flavours and we gathered round him. "Mind you," he began, "you're dealing with all fruit flavours, think of the variety — the blackcurrant, the gooseberry, the raspberry and above all what about the good, old-fashioned strawberry?" Why the strawberry should be termed old fashioned we never discovered. Each soap, and there were many of them, seemed in the course of time to become associated with a certain type of copy. Around Puritan Soap there gathered a certain homespun aura. It was full of housewifely allusions — all very honest-to-goodness, solid value and what-Mother-Brown-says, sort of stuff. Lifebuoy Soap was tackled in the heroic manner — a very expansive and grandiose style. I can remember the opening lines of one of my efforts, which they continued to use for at least a year. It began "No victorious army, no navy that

UNEMPLOYED! UNEMPLOYABLE?

ever sailed the seven seas has claimed so many victims as man's eternal enemy — DIRT". For Easy Shaving Stick I let myself go on a would-be humorous line which gained much favourable comment. Later on I branched into verse, one piece ended :

> Reggie, dear, your beard does prick.
> Please use Easy Shaving Stick.

Sometimes the Copy Pool waited several days without being called upon to put pen to paper. On one well-remembered occasion we waited a whole week without being called upon. Until late on Saturday morning (we worked on Saturdays in those days) just as we were packing up to leave, a request for some copy came through. A few harsh things were said about the management.

One story, which I believe to have a basis in fact, concerned a washing soap which was very popular in the North. It was a yellow soap with a blue mottle which was there by accident. At last some genius found a way, in the course of its manufacture, of removing the mottle. Much rejoicing! Unfortunately the public set great store on the efficiency of the mottle and sales dropped at an alarming rate. Meanwhile they had forgotten how the original mottle was produced. After much experiment and great expenditure they found a means of re-introducing the mottle artificially.

Palmolive Soap had made a great name for itself in America and Lever Brothers thought it would pay them to introduce a similar line to the British public. They called their version — Olva. An old friend of mine who was working with me at the time remembers the first two sentences introducing this new line :

> Say Olva, and if necessary say Olva again; it is worth a little insistence to get the only pure palm and olive soap.

Part of our training consisted of a month at Port Sunlight. During this spell I went and lived with my brother, who at that time was on the Baltic in Liverpool. Port Sunlight was the first signpost to the Welfare State as applied to private enterprise. Undoubtedly, industrially speaking, it was an enormous breakthrough — a brain-child of the first Lord Leverhulme. The workers were housed well, near to their factory, and had everything laid on and close at hand. There was a shopping centre, a picture gallery, cinemas and halls for dancing and other entertainment. I have no doubt it was, and is, considered a godsend by the Lever Brothers employees. I fear I was too individualistic to appreciate it. To live alongside those with whom you worked and met every day is my idea of hell, and I am a very gregarious individual.

On my return to London I rejoined the Copy Pool for a few months, until one day I learned that I was going to join another department and in a few days found myself in the financial department, where they seemed to occupy the time by buying and selling foreign exchange. I simply didn't understand what it was all about and no one took the trouble to explain it to me. Looking back I realize that I should have enquired the reason for their shifting me. I rather thought they were trying to give me a general view of the whole organization. It never occurred to me to question their wisdom. In about a month's time I was moved again. This time it was to "go on the road" in an effort to sell, oh horrors, a baby food which an astonishingly small number of people seemed to want and, therefore, rather naturally nobody bought. This was certainly the most depressing and futile quest I ever encountered.

For one week I was packed off to Bristol to man a stand at some sort of pharmaceutical exhibition. I can remember only one incident connected with that dreary week. A friend of mine on the stand confided that he had found a tailor who would make to measure a coat and a pair of plus-fours for forty-five shillings. I chose the material. They took my measurements and asked me to call for a fitting in two days' time. I returned as arranged, stepped into the plus-fours and put on the coat. Quite by chance I put my hand in one of the pockets and finding a small piece of paper, pulled it out and read it. A brief message had been scribbled — "Keep stitches in for mock try-on tomorrow." In fact the whole visit was a complete waste of time. I never revealed to those tailors my discovery of their guile. After all, what could you expect for forty-five bob?

A few days after my return to London I received a note to the effect that the company had decided to dispense with my services. This was a stunning blow. I asked for and obtained an interview with Will Lever, who was very kind and sympathetic but informed me that they had concluded that I had failed to show sufficient promise.

On my return from Port Sunlight I had written a light-hearted piece of nonsense of my experiences. In this article I happened to compare the stacks of maturing red Lifebuoy Soap to models of a street of New York skyscrapers lit by the setting sun. I introduced various other fanciful theories and allusions, and sent it in to a trade journal which dealt exclusively with soap, its manufacture and its sale. It was accepted. A few weeks after my departure, I was told that one of the Lever Brothers directors, I think his name was Walls, who dealt with advertising, was complaining that he was surrounded by a lot of duds with absolutely no imagination. "You never seem to have any ideas," he complained. "Now look here," he said picking up the soap journal and pointing to my article. "Here is someone with real imagination. Someone who holds the reader's attention. Why can't I collect people like the author of this story, then we should be going places." With great relish one of my friends put up his hand. "Please, sir, it may interest you to know that the author in question was in your employ until a fortnight ago when you sacked him." Silence reigned.

I had made one very good friend in the Lever Brothers Copy Pool — a gay, delightful Irish girl who went by the name of Mrs. Colbert. She was one of the most beautiful and attractive women it has ever been my good fortune to know. Kay Colbert had been through an unfortunate marriage and was at that time friendly with Francis Vanden Heuvel, a man she was destined to marry in the space of a year or so. Van as he was invariably called, was busy reviving the fortunes of the Eno's Fruit Salt Company, which he did with enormous success. As it happened, he occupied offices in the same building at Blackfriars in which I had been working.

"Why don't you go and see Van," she suggested. I did. Almost immediately we seemed to be on terms of a close and lasting friendship. "I think you ought to be in a small advertising agency. Why don't you go along and see Pem." He took out a visiting card and on it he wrote "I should like you to meet my friend Oliver Nickalls". "Pem" turned out to be Alfred Pemberton, the son of Max Pemberton and a godson of Lord Northcliffe. He took me on at the figure I asked for, £300 a year. It was a fruitful and happy union. In about fifteen years I had worked my way up and with him had become part-proprietor of the firm of Alfred Pemberton Ltd. It was an ideal and very successful partnership, and we worked happily together until we sold our respective interests in the business nearly forty years later.

Chapter 12

I Deserve To Be Hung

EVER since I can remember I have derived intense pleasure from colour and this passion impelled me at a very early age to cover numerous pieces of paper with crude drawings in coloured chalks and with the brightest colours that I could find in my water-colour box. For some unknown reason, however, among small boys of the Edwardian era, it was considered effete to take art seriously. Mr. Wright, art master at my preparatory school, was one of the most gloriously ineffective teachers I have ever met. Chaos reigned throughout his lessons and the poor man had not the ghost of an idea of keeping order.

When I moved on to Eton I found that the art classes were still slumbering in a Victorian twilight; but after the First World War standards improved. Eric Powell (who as a master there had won the Diamond Sculls in 1912) had, on the outbreak of war, joined the Royal Flying Corps to find that, quite by chance, he was no mean artist; in the absence of cartridge paper, many of his first efforts were done on the material which was used at that time to cover the wings of aircraft.

A year or so before going up to Oxford, I had bought some oil paints and their accompanying accessories and thought I'd see what I could do on my own account. At the moment when I seemed ready to start I found that I had failed to buy a canvas. But the mood was on me and I refused to be daunted. I went and foraged in the outhouses adjoining our home. There I was lucky enough to find an old rabbit hutch with a three-ply door hanging on its hinges. I ripped it off; dusted it down and went to work. My first attempt was a self-portrait. I made faces at myself in a looking glass. This, I had decided, was not going to be a straightforward affair, but something pretty horrific. I scowled at myself, bared my teeth, and assumed an evil expression of malice and hatred. I set to work in some discomfort. It was difficult for my features to hold the expression. The particular contortions I had decided upon made my face ache considerably. Such was the discomfort that I was forced to relax every minute or so. When at length I had finished I was really rather pleased with myself, "not half as bad as I had expected". If anyone should show sufficient interest to demand a title, I would reply, for no very good reason, "Communism".

Following on that first attempt, I laid in a stock of canvas and, in the course of a month or so, found myself drawn towards landscape.

At the same time, I would, whenever I got the chance, tramp round various art exhibitions. Looking back I realize that these visits were not so much to admire the pictures as to note the way various artists produced various affects; and my old friend George Drinkwater, himself an artist, who never seemed to have made the name for himself which he deserved, gave me excellent advice. It was he who revealed to me, amongst other things, the possibility of using Essex (or S-X) wall boarding in place of canvas. Not only is it considerably cheaper, but it offers a splendid surface which is entirely suitable for the reception of oil paints and to my mind far more satisfying than canvas of whatever texture or graining.

Two darling old spinster aunts of mine who lived together were a constant and valuable help. Maud, the younger one, was a good artist, and painted boldly — more, dare I say it? — like a man than like a woman. Her style had much in common with that of the late Dame Laura Knight. Grace had taken up painting late in life, more as a means of self-defence against her sister's unflagging energy than for any other reason.

I remember joining my aunts for a sketching holiday in Cornwall. They were staying at Lamorna — such a lovely place as I remember it then. Whilst there we were invited up

I DESERVE TO BE HUNG

to his studio by Lamorna Birch. He had, so I understand, given himself the name of Lamorna, not merely because he happened to live there but to distinguish himself from another painter of the same surname. I remember being extraordinarily impressed by that visit. He had some lovely work in hand. At that particular time he was, I think, at his zenith as an artist. In later life I felt that his work became tighter, harder and somehow too glittering, as compared to his pictures of his earlier period.

One evening I was painting a beach scene in which an upturned rowing boat figured prominently. Below the waterline it had, at some time, been painted red. Out came my tube of vermilion and I slashed it on in an orgy of indiscretion. I showed it to my aunts. "My dear," exclaimed Maud. "You shouldn't have used all that raucous red. I know why you used it. You think that red is a warm colour whereas in fact vermilion is a cold colour. Now the bottom of that boat is a nice warm, faded crimson colour, rather the same shade . . . " and here she pointed to her sister " . . . as the tip of Grace's nose."

The book written by Winston Churchill I think caps all the literature which has been published on sketching and painting. Particularly do I like his description of the time when he had just taken up painting. He was sitting brush in hand, poised in trepidation before a blank, snow-white canvas, when Lady Lavery strolled up from behind him. "Painting?" she enquired. "Well, what are you waiting for?" and seizing his brush, she dipped it into the oil and then into the blue. Drawing a well-charged brushful across the top of the canvas she explained, "There's your sky. Now you can get on with it!" This taught him, he continues, one important lesson—that when in doubt err on the side of boldness.

How true that is. Some of my less disappointing efforts have happened as a result of my attacking the canvas in a fury of creative fervour. Often, when painting, I have found myself facing a wind so strong that the canvas, if not the whole easel, has started to tip towards me. On such occasions, I adopt an aggressive, fencing attitude and lunging towards the tottering mass, force it back to the perpendicular with the tip of my brush.

I am so much in sympathy with Van Gogh. Once, as a student, he was painting so fiercely that the paint was dripping off the canvas on to the floor. His teacher, in a fury, remonstrated with him; whereupon he stood back, fixed his mentor with an angry stare and shouted, "I am Vincent the Dutchman", as though that in itself was sufficient justification. The sequel is not quite so happy for it is recorded, "However, he was put back to the drawing class."

I wonder how many painters there are who really appreciate that poem by Rudyard Kipling which opens with the line "When earth's last picture is painted". Often I quote it to myself. I have a special affection for the lines.

> And they that were good shall be happy
> They shall sit in a golden chair
> And splash at a ten league canvas
> With brushes of comet's hair.

"Brushes of comet's hair." What a magnificent concept. Sometimes in one of my dottier moments, I plan for the whole poem to be set to music. I can almost hear it as an unaccompanied choral number for male voices. It would become the National Anthem for artists, to be used only on special occasions such as the Royal Academy banquet. When, however, my sanity returns I realize it would never do. Some of you may remember the lines from the same poem which read:

> They shall have real saints to draw from
>   Magdalen, Peter and Paul
> They shall work for an age at a sitting and
>   Never get tired at all.

Can you imagine the fury and disgust amongst some of the more modern and less representational artists at the thought of having "real saints to draw from"? It would quite spoil their evening!

Through the years I continued my holiday painting in a desultory way. It certainly never occurred to me to stage an

I DESERVE TO BE HUNG

exhibition, nor did I ever send in my work to any society or group. I never thought I was in that class. It so happened, however, that during the last war when at Henley-on-Thames in the somewhat bewildering position of a platoon commander in the Home Guard, one evening, after I had dismissed the platoon, one of my corporals came up to me and said that on occasions he had noticed me at some of his exhibitions. He turned out to be Leger of the Leger Galleries in Bond Street.

I invited him up to dinner and bridge at a council house I had rented in Henley. Quite by chance I had a recent sketch of mine hanging on the wall. It was a cherry tree in full blossom (not half as grossly sentimental as it may sound). It didn't take much encouragement for me to reveal it as a "poor thing but mine own". He asked me if I had ever exhibited. "Good God, no," I replied. "I'm simply not in that class." "I can't think why you say that. Call in at my office tomorrow morning and I'll tell you what to do." I kept the appointment, and at my third attempt I was hung at the Burlington House Summer Exhibition. For the uninitiated I should explain that pictures submitted for inclusion at the Summer Exhibition are either accepted, or refused outright or accepted and yet not hung. Some people have a curious notion that once a picture is refused, it must not be resubmitted. This is not the case. An artist is allowed to submit the same picture as often as he likes. Should any picture of mine be accepted and not hung, I invariably send it in again the following year. One of my paintings was hung at its fifth appearance before the selectors. It had been refused twice; accepted and unhung twice, and hung the following year. You never know your luck. But all that was many years ago. Since then I have been hung on various occasions, though I refuse to reveal the exact number, leaving the reader to guess whether such reticence stems from modesty or shame.

Varnishing Day is a misnomer for the last thing that exhibitors seem to do is to varnish. Usually it seems to be a sort of mutual admiration society with the exhibitors playing a lovely game of "I'll look at your picture, if you'll look at mine". And there, with arms linked, they stroll in couples from picture to picture. Once I was caught in the act of varnishing by that darling doyen of seascape painters — Norman Wilkinson. "Young man," he said, "you should never varnish a picture until it has been painted for at least three or four years." "That's all very well for you chaps, you paint for posterity," I replied. "But no one's going to give a damn about this picture after it leaves these walls and so I'm going to make it look as good as possible while it's here."

It was after being very seriously ill. I was still very weak and in a highly emotional state when my wife came in and remarked, "Something rather nice has happened to you." "I haven't been accepted by the Academy?" I asked. "You have," she said. Whereupon I burst into floods of tears. She handed me a card. Good God! I was on the line! Would the hospital authorities allow me to attend Varnishing Day? Not if there were a lot of people there but I could go along if I could arrange a private visit. I rang up Henry Carr and asked him if he could help. "What is the number of your picture?" he asked. I gave it him. "What an astonishing thing," he exclaimed. "They entrusted the hanging of that room to me and I assure you I hadn't the slightest idea that you had sent in anything. Leave it all to me." I was dropped at Burlington House at the appointed hour and Henry had arranged for an attendant with a bathchair to meet me in the entrance hall. I was wheeled into the lift, hoisted to the right floor and propelled towards my picture. Suddenly my wife, pointing to another wall, exclaimed, "There's another picture of yours!" She'd failed to show me the original notice of its acceptance and to have two accepted and hung was almost too good to be true.

What this chapter is meant to convey is that I am an enthusiastic if indifferent painter; though the sheer joy and fun I have experienced, in practice, and in pursuit of improvement is beyond all price.

Chapter 13

Three Characters In Search of an Author

Dr. *Winnington Ingram (Bishop of London)*

I FIND myself sorely tempted to write about three characters whose personalities have left a lasting impression on me, either on account of what they have done, said or written. It was Oscar Wilde who wrote that the only way to get rid of temptation was to give way to it and I intend to do exactly this.

My first subject is Dr. Arthur Foley Winnington Ingram, for thirty-eight years Bishop of London. I had heard him preach when I was convalescent on Malta—the occasion being the first Armistice Sunday, in 1918. I met him for the first time just over two years later, in 1921, when I was in training for the Boat Race at Putney. It was his custom, and a very kind custom it was, to entertain the crews to luncheon at Fulham Palace. We were ushered towards the presence and suddenly there he was, standing with what I believe in ecclesiastical circles is known as a Canterbury cap on his head, in a sort of somewhat claustrophobic cul-de-sac. On our arrival, exuding bonhomie, he advanced with outstretched, all-embracing arms, to welcome us. "Boys, boys, welcome to Fulham Palace. I had better tell you right away that I have a number of curates and their wives to meet you. So you'll have a lady and a curate each. Next week I have the Cambridge crew coming. I have five bishops for them. I should think they'll have a fit."

It was Pat Mallam who spoke first. "Please, Bishop," he pleaded, "do you think I could dispense with my curate and have two ladies." This was greeted with gales of laughter from the Bishop. "Come out into the garden," he commanded, and led the way. Having arrived at a certain vantage point, he stopped and announced, "You are now standing on the hockey field. Over there we have a squash court. We have an annual tournament. I may say that the Duke of York was knocked out in the second round last week."

Eventually we were all seated at luncheon. True to his word we had a curate and a lady on either side of us. The good lady on my right was in a reverential mood. She turned to me and in a subdued voice remarked, "Of course, just as some people say there is only one Prince of Wales, so we say there is only one Bishop of London." It would have been downright rude to have suggested that her remark was a glimpse of the obvious; especially as I knew exactly what she meant. Just as I was muttering assent, the Bishop, who had been in earnest conversation with the curate next to him, raised his voice and with outstretched hands, indicating the portraits on the walls, announced to the assembled company, "Boys, boys, all round the walls you will see portraits of all the Bishops of London," and then inviting us to gaze at one at the end of the line, he added, "The last and worst, your humble servant." In the years to come, I was to learn that this was a ploy he repeated quite regularly.

Later he confided to us that he was sometimes challenged on the question of teetotalism. A heckler once parried one of his remarks, asking how it came about that Cambridge were inclined to win the Boat Race when they trained on strong beer. To which his invariable reply was, "That may be so, but do you know what Oxford train on? They train on old port. I have no need to tell you that old port has a considerably higher alcohol content than strong beer."

Suddenly his parlourmaid offered some delicacy of the sort that was definitely forbidden by the rules of training as they were understood in those days. "Ellen, Ellen!" he reprimanded her. "You're spoiling me as usual. No, thank you. I'll have the same as the boys." This was certainly no very great hardship. "Robert, Robert!" he called to a muscular-looking curate at the far end of the table. "Don't you go and eat too much cheese down there." By way of

THREE CHARACTERS IN SEARCH OF AN AUTHOR

explanation, he added, "I'm playing squash with him at the Bath Club this afternoon."

I reminded him of his Armistice Sunday sermon back in 1918 and mentioned that I was present. "After lunch I will show you some of my photographs," he commented. "The Salonika boy can look at my Salonika photographs and the others can look at my naval photographs. I didn't tell you how I bumped the bottom with Holbrook V.C., did I?"

I lunched with him again either in 1922 or 1923, and then I did not meet him again for some fourteen years. In 1937 or 1938 I was coaching Oxford at Putney and once again found myself lunching at Fulham Palace. I was happy to note that the intervening years had used him well. He was as hale and hearty and as full of fun as ever. Meanwhile two stories had come to me concerning him.

Once on his arrival in New York, he was asked by a brash American reporter whether he intended to inspect any night clubs whilst he was in New York. With a twinkle in his eye the Bishop countered, "Are there any night clubs in New York?" This was too good an opportunity to be missed and a headline was splashed across the front page of a certain journal, "Bishop of London arrives. Asks 'Are there any night clubs in New York?'"

One day I was talking to a friend of mine who had no very high regard for Winnington Ingram. Did he call him a ghastly old humbug or a terrible man? I can't remember. He added that he could never forgive him for a certain remark. It appears that the Bishop was watching a game of lawn tennis when a dark threatening cloud appeared in the sky. A tiny tot of a girl ran up to him and pointing heavenwards lisped something regarding the possibility of a shower. "No, no, my dear," the Bishop is reputed to have said. "Even the Bishop of London can't stop the rain."

I remember my last meeting with him very well. His retirement was imminent. I asked him how he intended to pass the time. He didn't hesitate. "I shall tour the world for five years," he announced, "and then I shall be ready to tour the other world."

The Bishop was a keen fisherman and on one occasion I

succeeded in drawing him into giving me a graphic description of a tussle he had had with a salmon on the Avon which he had hooked on a Blue Charm. Apparently it took some time to land, and as proof of this he volunteered that the fight lasted so long that they had to feed him with sandwiches. I remarked that his exploit, as he described it, reminded me more of a channel swimmer than a fisherman. Curiously enough I knew the man who had been detailed to try to put him into a salmon. "The old boy was awfully keen on his rod," he remarked. "Told us that it was fifty years old. I must say it was an astonishing implement. It produced a sort of hingeing action about half way up as he cast. What astonished me was not that it was fifty years old but that it wasn't one hundred and fifty years old."

A distant relation of mine nourished an affection for the Bishop bordering on an obsession. Being a man of independent means he appointed himself to him as a sort of unofficial, unpaid A.D.C., and accompanied him on his various world tours. His name was Ormonde Blyth, and he was also related to the directors of the wine and spirit merchants W. & A. Gilbey. I brought up the subject of Ormonde. "Dear Ormonde," mused the Bishop. "He came in here the other night absolutely reeling. 'I'm not tight,' he assured me. 'I know you're not, I wish you were,' I said. Apparently some years back he suffered an accident at polo. It still affects him occasionally."

On the Bishop's recent Australasian tour Ormonde had done a lot of useful work on behalf of the family firm. As the Bishop travelled by train from town to town, his hosts took good care to see that he was provided with plenty of liquid refreshment to sustain him on the journey. Ormonde's family loyalty made certain that he was presented with Gilbey liquor. "The Bishop won't drink anything but Gilbey's," he would explain. On one occasion Winnington Ingram was explaining to a group of journalists how he relied on Ormonde to attend to all the details. "I have absolutely nothing to do," he added. "I just get in the train and sit tight." The following day the headlines announced "Bishop says 'I just sit in the train and get tight'."

THREE CHARACTERS IN SEARCH OF AN AUTHOR

I reminded the old man of his sermon in the cathedral at Valetta some twenty years previously. "I think you're the only person left now who remembers it," he sighed, as I said goodbye to him for the last time. Some four or five weeks later I was talking about the Bishop to a lady I had just met at a tennis-party. "That's extraordinary," she said. "A month or so ago I was told that I must make a point of hearing him preach; as he was retiring there wouldn't be many more chances. I remember parts of his sermon quite clearly. He said, 'Only the other day, I was talking to an old and valued friend of mine. He reminded me of what I had said in a sermon I preached in Valetta on that first Armistice Sunday so many years ago. And he told me what a great spiritual help something I had said on that occasion had been to him in the intervening years!'" That I had said no such thing is neither here nor there. Anyhow, who am I to deny that his words had proved "a great spiritual help"? He may have known me better than I knew myself—bless him.

Lady Harris

I first met Cara Harris in 1936. I had been on a fishing holiday in Iceland. The party consisted of my old friend Sebastian Earl, a mutual friend of our Oxford days by the name of Theo Turner, and Austin Harris, our senior by some thirty years. On our return Austin kindly asked my wife and myself to dine with him, and it was then that we were introduced to his wife Cara—the most astonishing and original woman I have ever met. After dinner she produced her scrapbook, and as she turned its pages she glanced not at the book which she knew well enough, but at my wife and myself. She was absolutely absorbed in noting our reactions to her collection. On one page she had pasted a press photograph of Queen Mary walking along in conversation with the Archbishop of Canterbury. Nothing very interesting about that, you may think, but a second glance revealed that there was something disturbingly awry with the Queen below the waist. From some other photograph our hostess had cut out the tight-clad legs and thighs of a ballet dancer and imposed them on the original photograph. The sight of Queen Mary wearing tights and with a broad smile on her face, walking with the beaming Archbishop of Canterbury was bizarre to say the least of it. Turning over the page and pointing to another of her twists in this vein she remarked, "I can never make up my mind whether that is a double or treble entendre," nor could we.

Cara Harris was a painter of some skill and originality. She arranged on one occasion to give an exhibition of her pictures. But an ordinary, straightforward exhibition would not do for Cara. So her lively imagination invented an unknown French painter who had died of tuberculosis at the age of twenty-one. She called him Rognons de la Flêche. She hired a gallery, crammed a treasure table with a number of alleged mementos of the poor young artist—a lock of hair, a pair of gloves, a walking stick, a faded buttonhole and other articles, and sat selling catalogues at the entrance to her exhibition. The pictures of course were her own, and what rapturous notices they received! "We are just beginning to realize what the art world has lost through the tragic and early death of Rognons de la Flêche," one of them opined.

I remember many of her pictures, one in particular of a nude young lady sitting up in bed holding up a fish by its tail. At the foot of her bed are grouped two robust-looking Scotsmen clad in rough tweeds and wearing glengarries. Should you enquire the exact significance of the picture or ask for an explanation, you were informed, "She's just showing them the fish she's caught."

Austin on one occasion insisted she give a dinner party consisting of various prominent and, to her mind, boring personalities. Cara made quite certain that the dinner would be an unqualified failure. Her son Peter was in the Brigade and she persuaded him to collect a few of his friends and wait at table. They were careful to see that their nails and hands were quite filthy, their hair unbrushed, whilst one of them wore a patch over one eye, and another one of those artificial finger stalls smudged with red paint to indicate blood. They tramped round the table in the heaviest

THREE CHARACTERS IN SEARCH OF AN AUTHOR

hobnail boots. Cara, in her wicked way, was delighted. What amused her was the sight of her horror-stricken guests pretending not to notice there was anything unusual.

On another occasion she gave a political party. During dinner she raised the question of the delights to be enjoyed from jumping about on a pogo stick—an unusual pastime, which was at that moment a popular craze. Not one of them had tried it. "You will after dinner," Cara promised them. Having hired a number of pogo sticks, she put on the gramophone and bade them jump. At one moment it is reported that several members of the Cabinet were jumping around her drawing-room like jack-in-the-boxes. "Don't they look rather ridiculous?" whispered Cara to a friend.

Each summer the Harris family migrated to their home on the Isle of Wight. On one occasion, thinking it rather nonsense that some of her neighbours there should have lists of their Cowes Week house-parties inserted in *The Times*, Cara sent in an entirely imaginary one of her own. It read, "Sir Austin and Lady Harris are entertaining . . ." The first guests on her list lent a "feathered friends" atmosphere, they were "The Dean of Orpington and Mrs. Wyandotte". In after years Austin declared it to be a most unfortunate mistake. He affirmed, quite untruthfully I suspect, that it turned out that there actually was a Dean of Orpington, from whom they received an angry letter denying that he had been one of their guests over Cowes Week.

On the evening we were there, they decided to show us a home-made movie of quite exceptional brilliance. Cara was cast in the part of Dame Tarchtre, who intends to go in search of her sister who years before had mysteriously disappeared in darkest Africa. The opening shots included a finger pointing to photographs of a number of topless native women. At last the finger comes to rest on a particularly revolting specimen whose withered breasts looked as though they were in constant use as strops for cut-throat razors. "I feel sure that is Effie" ran the subcaption.

The next shot showed her departure for Africa. A paddle steamer which normally plied between Hyde and the mainland had been hired for the occasion, and Dame Tarchtre with some astonishing looking luggage, a badly rolled gamp in one hand and a parrot in a cage in the other, with much ado climbs on board. Her solitary figure standing in the stern and waving forlornly as the boat noses its way out to sea was a most effective sequence.

Once the Dame arrived in Africa a close-up of a cat stalking through a garden of bamboos represented a cross-section of the fierce animals she encountered on her safari. The closing scenes depicted Cara now lightly clad as a cannibal chieftain, earrings, nose-rings, a spear and all the expected accoutrements, attending her stewpots. On either side of her were steaming urns in which the chieftain was cooking his victims. This was a remarkable performance. Every now and then she would dip a finger into one of the urns, suck it appreciatively, and brandishing her spear, dance for joy and leap into the air at the prospect of the meal to come. I don't think Effie was ever found, but in Cara Harris I had found an amazing woman for whom age meant absolutely nothing — one who, I think, could be quite truthfully termed "the last of the great eccentrics".

Noel Arnott

One Sunday soon after we were married, my wife and I took a train to Taplow to lunch with her parents. A big, blond, clean-shaven man entered the compartment and sat down opposite us.

My wife and I are very averse to entering into random conversation with total strangers in trains, they can be so boring. That, however, was to be the exception which proves the rule. We soon learned that our companion was going down to lunch with some close friends of ours near Taplow. That evening, quite by chance, we returned on the same train to London. It was not long before we found we had much in common, and in the course of conversation he revealed himself as a devotee of opera. I can still remember his amusement when my wife, intending to refer to "Rheingold", mistakenly dubbed it "The Gold Rush" — a Charlie Chaplin film which was delighting audiences at the time.

THREE CHARACTERS IN SEARCH OF AN AUTHOR

Before we had reached Paddington we had mutually concluded that we would like to see some more of one another. His name turned out to be Noel Arnott, a bachelor who was to become almost our closest and most valued friend—one whom, except during the war years, we were to meet at least once a week until he died at the age of eighty, some forty years later.

He was a man immaculately dressed, extremely well-read, a great lover of music (*Rosenkavalier* being his favourite opera) and a keen follower of the Turf with an intimate knowledge of its history. He combined a lightness of touch and a dry wit with a certain restrained bawdiness of mind, which amused us. His yearning for the more spacious living of a former era showed itself in many little ways. He once admitted that had he sufficient funds he would invest in an electric brougham. On being asked the reason for this astonishing ambition, he replied—"When you go out in the evening, they've got so much more headroom. You can get in and out without having to take off your top hat." On taking his seat in a theatre, he would throw back his black, vermilion lined evening cloak, clasp his hands over the top of a gilt-knobbed cane which he held between his knees, and on being presented with a programme would exclaim, "Now let's see what it's all about!" Except towards the end of his life he was usually pressed for money, yet somehow he managed to retain the exclusive services of an Irish manservant who rejoiced in the name of Turner.

Almost invariably he left London for weekends in the country, and it so happened that the name of his host or hostess would almost certainly figure in Debrett. He would never agree with my suggestion that he was the most "gorgeous old snob". His definition of a snob, he would emphasize, was someone who preferred talking to a dull peer than an amusing commoner. When I suggested once that were he given the choice between an amusing peer and an amusing commoner, he would choose the peer, he retorted, "Who wouldn't."

In one of his "Ego" books of reminiscences, the late James Agate summed him up in the following paragraph:

"Dined with Noel Arnott. He is the last of the dandies. Every evening his manservant removes his shoe laces, irons them and replaces them in his shoes. Said of a well-known gold digger "the sort of woman who ought to be strung up and thrashed with wet holly, but not a woman to dine with or talk to".

Noel was the youngest child of a large family. His father, for whom he cherished a great affection and a life-long admiration, was at one time the Dean of Rochester. Noel must have sorely tried the patience of this long-suffering man. So often had he had to stump up for him and tide him over some financial crisis that, as far as Noel was concerned, his last Will and Testament made depressing reading. Every sentence, so he confided to me, ended with the words " . . . and this shall apply to all my children, excepting my youngest son Noel". He certainly never blamed his father for making these distinctions; on the contrary he readily admitted that he deserved them. He once explained our widely divergent attitudes to our respective homes. "You," he said, "were fortunate in having parents who attuned themselves to modern ideas and loved having your friends to stay with them. Mine, in spite of my love for them, remained boringly Victorian and so my one ambition was to get away from home."

He was educated at Dulwich. His early manhood seems to have consisted of being sent to some job overseas, of returning after one or two years, only to get into some scrape or other and be packed off abroad once again. At one period of his life he was in the Rhodesian Mounted Police, and in time rose to be secretary or personal assistant to various governors.

On his return home he took various civilian jobs, yet was never successful in earning more than a modest competence. A few years prior to the outbreak of war he was taken by Packards, installed in an elegant office in Berkeley Street, where he was successful in selling their cars to many of his well-to-do, influential friends. On the outbreak of war it became obvious that there was no future in the automobile market. He was now approaching fifty, yet somehow or other

THREE CHARACTERS IN SEARCH OF AN AUTHOR

he managed to get himself into the Army. He had been wounded fighting in Africa during the First World War. His left arm was badly shattered which left it slightly incapacitated for the rest of his life. At that time he never took a commission, though as a ranker he must have distinguished himself in some way or other, for he was one of the very few Englishmen to have been awarded the *Medaille Militaire*. His "medical" for the Second World War cannot have been very stringent, for he was accepted, given a commission, and within a few months was once more on his way to Africa.

He was a good correspondent and his letters contained many colourful descriptions of his doings, as well as a host of witty remarks on his experiences. We were soon to learn that he had somehow wangled himself a job as an A.D.C. to Sir Miles Lampson in Cairo. My comment was that he must surely be the oldest A.D.C. in captivity. He wrote that it was extremely difficult to train the native servants to wait satisfactorily at table, and described in detail the lengths he had to go to to prevent their spilling hot soup on what he described as the prematurely bald pate of some visiting bigwig. Winston Churchill arrived to stay at the Embassy and Noel was consulted as to the best way of plying him with champagne at dinner, a luxury which it was felt need not be extended to the whole party. He devised a scheme whereby all the wine was put into glass jugs. One jug only contained champagne. It was marked by a little circle of bright red paper stuck on to the handle in an inconspicuous position — that was reserved for Churchill. All the other jugs were unmarked and filled with a sparkling white burgundy.

Churchill had just been on a visit to Stalin, and was wearing a boiler suit. He was wondering what little present he could send Stalin as a mark of esteem. Lady Lampson suggested, "Why not give him one of your boiler suits?" "I shall have to give him a good deal more than that to satisfy him," replied Churchill. He then went on to describe a form of punishment which he declared our Soviet allies meted out to their military malefactors, "They remove their nether garments, fling them on to the ice and leave them there until the morning", and then turning to Lady Lampson, he enquired, "How would you like that, my good lady?"

One day we received a letter from Noel which transcended all the others. Having referred to Lampson as an unappreciative master, he continued, "However, I have made one good friend out here and as it happens to be Alexander, the Commander-in-Chief, it is just as well for me in that when I am flung or fling myself from the uneasy trapeze of A.D.C.dom, he will probably see that a resilient net in the form of a soft army job is set to catch me." He continued, "Spent three days with him in his caravan in the Western Desert. Most interesting. Did some sea bathing. The last time I had allowed my delicious body to be lowered into the Mediterranean was at Charlie's Mount (Monte Carlo) to the sound of music and surrounded by delicious and easily-persuaded women. How different from the scrawny, venereal Bedouin with lice on their bodies and camel's dung in their hair."

One day on his return to this country I was quoting this passage to him. "Say it again," he commanded. "Why should I?" I enquired. "After all it was you who wrote it." "I know, I know," he answered. "But it sounds so much better when you say it than when I wrote it."

His attitude towards Turner, his manservant, would have shocked anyone who had not been forewarned. He adopted a severe, reprimanding approach which had long since become an act — a duologue put on for the benefit of anyone who happened to be present. Turner entered into the spirit of such entertainment and though Noel meant every word he said, he put it over in such a way that Turner never bore him any grudge. He remained smiling and happy.

We went to dine with him one evening in his small house in Ellis Street. Noel had been out and hadn't as yet returned. Turner was busy cleaning up his shoes and felt that he was called upon to engage us in conversation and to make us feel at home. Noel returned and having greeted us, turned to Turner. "Now what are you doing? Boring the pants off my guests as usual I suppose." "Oh, sorry," retorted Turner with a broad grin, and then branched into a mumbo-jumbo of explanation only to be interrupted by his employer. "Now that will be quite enough of that, Turner. D'you mind getting straight back to the servants' hall where you belong, my good man." Turner, still smiling, sloped off into the kitchen, a small room about eight by six feet.

On occasions when Noel went away for the weekend, he would seek permission to bring Turner with him. "Chiefly so that he can replenish my wine glass at dinner," as he explained. Motoring down with him, Turner would usually receive a lecture on the way he was to behave. "Now, Turner, I would rather you didn't get up and sing songs in the servants' hall after supper." "And that I never do, sorr," exclaimed Turner. "Oh, yes, you do. I've had complaints about it. You must understand that the singing of songs after supper may have been all very amusing in the Sergeants' Mess twenty or thirty years ago, but nowadays, with the introduction of radio, people are bored stiff with it. I'd rather you desisted. D'you understand?" Turner understood perfectly, and what is more never showed the least resentment at being addressed in this *ex cathedra* fashion.

One morning Noel rang me up. Would I go down to lunch with him at Woburn, as his friend Ian Bedford wanted my advice about advertising the attractions of Woburn. I agreed to go, adding something to the effect that there was very little I could teach the Duke about advertising. On our arrival, our host asked if we would like a drink. "Of course," said Noel. "It's a dry martini, isn't it?" asked the Duke. "Well, you know where everything is, Noel. You had better go and mix it for yourself." Noel went off into the next room and Bedford turned to me. "I used to offer Noilly Prat for making dry martinis, but Noel tells me that's very common. I must offer Dry Martini, so Dry Martini it is."

On one occasion Noel was spending his annual holiday with friends in Brittany. He wrote admitting he was bored and getting fed up with being asked to admire the lace-making Bretons, in their quaint caps. "I rather care for the village postmistress, aged sixteen, with the most beautiful hands. I buy my stamps from her every day. Any moment now I intend asking her up to my room. I simply can't wait to show her my three-cornered Mauritius."

Chapter 14

I Get That Sinking Feeling

I BELIEVE that the chance, however slim, of oarsmen ending in the river, rather than on the river, accounts for a goodly percentage of the attendance at regattas and boat races. The crowd thoroughly enjoys an accident, and the possibility that oarsmen may end up "in the drink" is almost irresistible. I was the victim of one such accident in a pair-oar and cannot exaggerate the popularity of that particular mishap. It occurred many years ago, but even today people come up to me not so much to discuss a victory or hard-fought race, but to hear my version of this affair.

"Tell us about the time you sank," is the opening gambit. I intend therefore to quote the official description of this race. The fact that the compiler of those annals has seen fit to report it at greater length than any other single race in the history of Henley Regatta lends some weight to the theory that I have expressed above; that the crowd would rather see people swimming by accident than rowing in earnest. The record reads as follows:

The Silver Goblets and Nickalls Challenge Cup
Thursday, 3rd July

5.25 p.m.   Heat 2

Bucks.			Berks.		
G. K. Hampshire, bow	strs	10 2	G. O. Nickalls, bow	strs	12 1 3
W. Phillips, str		12 3	R. S. C. Lucas, str		13 06
(Magd. Coll. Ox.)			(Leander Club)		

The result of this race was entirely unexpected for Nickalls and Lucas were considered the probable winners of the Goblets. It was not generally known, however, that as well as famous oarsmen they were no mean amateur carpenters and always carried a set of tools. Whilst waiting at the Start, Stroke, thinking that the boat was unnecessarily heavy, cut away some of the bigger timbers and on the first stroke of the race Bow pushed his stretcher through the skin and she started to leak.

However, they soon took the lead and before going far, Hampshire and Phillips hit the booms and Nickalls and Lucas waited for them.

On re-starting Nickalls and Lucas again took the lead and were a long way ahead at Fawley, reached in 5.30. Here it became obvious that something was wrong for the boat was floating lower and lower in the water. In spite of the handicap they kept well ahead and it became more of a race against the leak than against their opponents. At the Mile Post it was clear that the leak was gaining on them fast and at the bottom of the Enclosure the cut-water disappeared and then the boat sank amidst execrations that were visible but inaudible at the Winning Post.

All this time Hampshire and Phillips were entirely unconscious of what had happened to their opponents whom they had not seen since about half way up the Island. When they came up with them they were not a little surprised to find them swimming and so stopped rowing. Ultimately they paddled in to complete the Course in 12.0 and immediately offered to row the race again. The Committee, however, could not allow this, pointing out that as they had passed the Winning Post the race was over and that a boat must abide by its accidents.

By the way, to those who wonder why the trophy for the Henley pair-oared event bears my name I should explain that there was no Challenge Cup for the event until my grandfather presented one in 1896 to commemorate the fact that his sons Guy and Vivian had, either with another partner or together, won the event for the previous six years. Altogether my surname appears on the silver plaques on the base of this Challenge Cup no less than thirteen times.

The official description of the race, quoted above, makes such good reading that I would not, if I could, have it altered in any way. It is not, however, entirely accurate. It is

I GET THAT SINKING FEELING

true that Lucas never embarked without a hammer and a file. It was seldom that the oar behaved to his liking. A few blows with the hammer on the leather button of his oar or some slight filing of his thole pin or oar handle seemed, for a time, to quieten his nerves, though it was not usually very long before the tools were again brought into action.

Lucas was a man of immense power; quite the strongest man with whom I have ever rowed. At the start of a race I had the greatest difficulty in holding him and keeping the boat straight. To make this easier I concluded that it would help if I could give myself more leverage by moving myself a few more inches into the bows. To accomplish this our boatman had found it necessary to remove the bulkhead. This is a slat of wood which, should any water be shipped into the well of the boat, prevents it running up the boat underneath the bow canvas. The crying shame was that, having removed the bulkhead the boatman, to save himself trouble, had failed to replace it. On the first stroke my stretcher broke away making a serious gash in the side of the boat through which green water poured in. If this had resulted in filling only the well of the boat we should have been all right, unfortunately, with no bulkhead to contain it, the water percolated right up to the bows. Opposite the Enclosures I turned round to see how low we were in the water and to my horror noticed that the forward canvas was gliding along under water. It wasn't even breaking the surface. The next stroke we went down by the bows in a most spectacular manner—for, as the bows descended into the watery depths so the stern reared itself most impressively some ten feet into the air.

That is the correct version of the affair. It is not true to say that we had sawn away some bigger timbers. It was very sporting of our opponents to offer to re-row the race. But then they were two very charming men whom we knew well. Hampshire had the distinction of rowing Head of the River and of taking a First in Chemistry in the same term. He eventually became a Director of I.C.I. and fathered that beautiful and talented actress, Susan Hampshire. Wogan Phillips, his partner, I remember as a most attractive personality. At one time he was married to that great writer Rosamond Lehmann, whom without ever hinting at my passion, I had known and worshipped from afar ever since we were children. Wogan, now Lord Milford, has, I believe, the distinction — if that is the word — of being the only Communist peer.

My father who was, I suppose, the most successful oarsman of all time, was very wise in his upbringing of his two sons. Obviously he was desperately keen that we should follow in his footsteps, yet he kept this to himself and never forced it upon us. Had we chosen some other form of sport he would have been perfectly content.

My father's Henley victories of 1905, 1906 and 1907 remain outstanding memories. I think it was in the latter year that my small brother and I were put into a gig and rowed our grandmother down the course. She was certainly the proudest grandmother at that Regatta. In the May of 1908 I went to my preparatory school. The Olympic Games were in London and Henley was chosen as the venue of the first Olympic Regatta. Rowing at that time had not spread to the four corners of the earth, and so to make up the entries it was agreed that each country should be allowed to enter two crews for each event. One of the United Kingdom's eight-oared crews was the winning Cambridge crew of that year, stroked by the redoubtable Douglas Stuart; while the other, a Leander crew, was to be composed of more mature oarsmen who had proved themselves in the past. Much to his delight, my father was asked to make himself available for this crew and eventually he was selected for what came to be known as "The Old Man's Crew". It turned out to be one of the fastest eights of all time. To give some idea of the variation in age, my father, who was then in his forty-first year, had rowed his first race at Henley before the stroke of his crew — one "Togo" Bucknall — was born.

The Belgians, it so happened, had put our rowing to shame and had carried all before them by winning the Grand Challenge Cup at Henley in the three previous years. This was obviously going to be my father's last aquatic appearance, and the Headmaster of my prep school, rather

I GET THAT SINKING FEELING

grudgingly I gather, gave his consent to my going home a week early to be present. Leander, having beaten first the Hungarians and then the Canadians, the final against the redoubtable Belgians proved to be an occasion I can never forget. There was the nervous tension prior to the start, the sickening anxiety during the race as my mother, through her field glasses, scanned the signal boxes bordering the course which indicated the relative positions of the crews. The glimmerings of hope when we learnt that Leander had taken the lead and the glorious, almost hysterical relief when they rowed in comparatively easy winners. It was about three hundred yards to the Leander raft from the Stand where we had been seated. My mother, a tiny little woman, gathered us together and told us to follow her. In an ecstasy of pride, she hurried up the towpath to greet and congratulate her husband. The crowd was already surging round the raft as Leander disembarked. Could we penetrate that mass of people? "I'm Mrs. Guy Nickalls," proclaimed my mother. A small man in the crowd took up the cry— "Make way for Mrs. Guy Nickalls" he shouted, as he charged through the crowd. "Make way for Mrs. Guy Nickalls." Another few seconds and we were on the raft. My mother and father went into an impassioned embrace. "Erstwhile" as one paper reported, "the proud sons clung round their father's knees."

Some twenty-five years ago I recorded in blank verse my impressions of those times—seen through the eyes of a small boy. They were originally published in a monthly magazine called *Courier*.

> Each year as I survey that wondrous scene,
> My mind drifts backwards nearly fifty years
> To the day when first I saw it.
> Lord! What an eyeful for a boy of five
> A cornucopia of sights and sounds,
> A visual feast of quivering impressions —
> Edwardian heydey, blue skies, pink champagne;
> The razzle dazzle of the parasol.

A RAINBOW IN THE SKY

And then later on, after describing the men's boaters and blazers, I recalled the fashions of the ladies:

> And then the ladies rather more restrained
> But nonetheless distinctly at their best,
> Bedecked in swinging, twinkling little jewels,
> Large hats perched high and lots of pale charmeuse,
> Or pink georgette all gathered at the waist
> And in cascading flounces falling to the ground.
> And as a background to this dazzling throng
> One hears a distant military band
> A thumping out the "Merry Widow" waltz
> And then with scarce a pause, "Pale Hands I loved",
> Rendered with gusto as a cornet solo.

But to return to my own progress as an oarsman. At the age of five or six I knew how to handle an oar, though I had to wait for a year or so to experience the thrill of propelling a light boat. Up to that time my rowing had been done in a gig, a dinghy, or one of those monstrous old craft known as a "randan". It was not until I went with my parents and younger brother to stay with the Ampthills at Milton Ernest, near Bedford, that I tasted the joys of propelling lighter more responsive craft. Lord Ampthill as I have recorded, had rowed with my father in their Oxford days. They had won the Goblets together at Henley and had been life-long friends. He was, moreover, my godfather and a jolly good godfather he turned out to be. Even as he walked to my christening, he confided to one of my aunts, who rather astonishingly happens to be with us still, that he had read up the duties of a godfather and had noticed that one of his chores was to take me to hear sermons. I am somewhat relieved to think that he never carried this into effect, though through the years he showed me a great many acts of kindness and affection.

It so happened that the River Ouse ran past the bottom of his garden. He had four sons of his own, two older and two younger than myself. He kept in his boathouse a coxed four and sculling boats of the type known as whiffs. They

I GET THAT SINKING FEELING

were clinker-built. This means that they were lightly constructed for speed, but with overlapping boards as opposed to fully-fledged racing boats where a thin wooden skin is steamed on to the skeleton of the boat. My brother Rodney and myself, together with Ampthill's two elder sons, Jack and Guy Russell, with their younger brother Eddie as cox, would man the four. Lady Ampthill had gone to the most enormous trouble to buy ribbons—light blue and dark brown. With these she trimmed rowing zephyrs in the approved fashion. Light blue and brown she informed us were the colours of the Milton Ernest Boat Club (the name of the village where they lived) and how proud we were of this insignia. Those were blissful days and it was then that I had my first experience of sculling in a whiff. In a few strokes I had found my balance and for the first time I took a stroke with all my power. It was a glorious sensation, the boat responded and sped on its way. Sheer ecstasy. Somehow I felt that it was analagous to archery, and that the boat could be compared to an arrow as it flew towards the gold. Is that too fanciful? Could it be compared to the satisfaction of driving a perfectly struck golf ball from the tee or, a sensation that has never come my way, of making a perfectly timed shot at racquets? I only knew that from that moment in so far as it was possible I was determined to excel.

I was a very small boy, and my first summer half found me—amongst other aquatic activities—coxing my Junior House Four, which took the form of bumping races, since disbanded I believe. At that time it had not been discovered that I was extremely short-sighted. The four ahead were within a few feet of bumping the boat immediately ahead of them. Immediate action was called for. Steering, as I had been instructed, my shortest course to the finish, I found the four we were chasing well out to my right. Pulling hard on my right rudder string I altered course and hit them amidships when they were within inches of bumping the crew in front of them. This was hailed as the most superb piece of coxing. I was somewhat bewildered, as the whole affair had been one of luck rather than good management. The result was that my second summer found me coxing the second

A RAINBOW IN THE SKY

eight. This didn't suit me at all. I was terrified that I should come to be regarded purely as a cox, whereas to become an efficient oarsman and sculler was my aim. As cox of an eight I was not very successful, the oars of my boat seemed in constant contact with the buttress of a bridge, or the bank. One of my severest critics was an Adonis of a young man by the name of Seagrave. At the outbreak of the 1914 War he joined the Royal Flying Corps and a few years later turned up with a broken ankle. He must have had a lucky escape, for it was generally understood that he had crashed from a considerable height. Later still he was to hold the land speed record, and years later I was very sad when I read of his death while attempting the water speed record on Lake Windermere.

As I have said, I had no wish to make my name as a cox and it came as something of a relief when on arriving on rafts one evening, I was informed by my successor that he had superseded me.

By 1916 my rowing had attracted sufficient attention for me to be given a trial for the Eton eight. I summoned all my powers. I concentrated assiduously on every stroke I rowed. Unlike my younger brother, to whom rowing came almost naturally, I realized that I should succeed only by the sweat of my brow and the application of such brains as I possessed. My brother, on the other hand, seemed to row naturally from the moment he was put in a boat. He gave the impression of possessing an experience well beyond his years. He was small of stature, yet this did not prevent him from stroking the school eight at the tender age of sixteen, when he was only a few pounds heavier than the cox.

I had to learn the hard way and envied him his astonishing aptitude. I failed to make the eight that year, and although I was included in the second eight I was bitterly disappointed. It affected my studies, and life became a bleak wasteland in spite of my being in the winning House Four, which gained a two-foot victory over a crew which included three members of the first eight. In my last summer term I succeeded, with Peter Kennedy, in winning the School Pulling (pair-oars). His father, Gilbert, had been a stalwart

I GET THAT SINKING FEELING

sculler of my father's generation, and I was included in the school eight at number seven. In the School Sculling I was beaten into second place by my pair-oared partner, but was once more successful in the House Fours. We won a private match against Shrewsbury School over the Henley course. In a few weeks' time I had joined a Cadet Battalion, not making another appearance on the river until 1919 when, suffering from post-malarial debilitation, I failed to distinguish myself in the Kingswood Sculls at the Henley Peace Regatta.

I have already recalled that on going up to Magdalen in the summer term of 1920, and from then on, I had more than my fair share of success. In the next nine years, in addition to minor victories I was President of the Oxford crew when it won in 1923. I gained two silver medals in the Olympic eight-oared event at Brussels and Amsterdam in 1920 and 1928, while at Henley I created a record by being in the winning Grand Challenge Cup crew on no less than seven occasions. With R. S. C. Lucas I gained two Goblet victories, and in 1928 rowing for the Thames Rowing Club I was successful in the Stewards Fours — my last race at Henley in which we got home by the narrow margin of one foot. In the twenty-four eight-oared races I rowed over the Henley course, the crew in which I was rowing were beaten only on two occasions.

It would be ludicrous to suggest that I failed to contribute to whatever success I may have enjoyed. But in this respect I cannot do better than paraphrase the words of my father when over forty years ago he wrote his autobiography. "I was fortunate in having some splendid men to row with me." Physically I was well endowed with an obstinacy or stubbornness above the average. This, in many respects, is an unattractive trait. It happens, however, to be a tremendous asset when it comes to any sort of competitive activity. I am quite certain that there are thousands of people who, given my opportunities, could have done much better. I rowed hard and I trained hard. There seems to be a general belief amongst the younger generation that we never really trained at all. This is completely untrue. When I had gone down from Oxford and had started in business, I had the greatest difficulty in keeping fit. I put on weight very easily. My rowing season would usually end with Henley Regatta at the beginning of July. In those years my rowing weight was 12st. 13lbs. By October it had risen to well over 14st. That was the moment when, with the next season in mind, I would start to get fit by running, skipping and various forms of physical jerks. I don't pretend that our training routine was as sophisticated as it is today. It did, however, succeed in getting rid of our superfluous poundage. Towards the end of my career, when my weight didn't seem to be responding to my strenuous endeavours, I consulted "Bossy" Phelps, a well-beloved boatbuilder, trainer and popular doyen amongst tideway watermen. His advice was, "You want to purge yourself, Mr. Gully. Take six or seven *cascaras* at one go. That will clean you out and give you a start on your weight reduction." Although I wouldn't recommend this drastic procedure to everyone, I'm bound to admit that it worked.

As I have said, I derived the utmost joy from my rowing. Not in any masochistic sense but in so many positive ways. The assuaging of a burning thirst; the satisfying of a giant appetite; the comfortable tiredness that presages a good night's sleep; the camaraderie of friends all set on the same objective. These things I loved. Then there was that wonderful feeling of fitness, the unleashing of a strength that seemed boundless, and then those wonderful days when the crew's improved technique brought a glorious response in the run and pace of the boat. What wouldn't I give to experience once again that controlled and steady swing forward just before one takes a perfectly timed and instantaneous beginning with a powerful application of work—a thrust that sends the boat speeding through the water. Those were the moments which brought such rich rewards. Sometimes it would seem almost as though the boat were a live thing which with its own particular brand of *joi de vivre*, was joining in the frolic by skidding through the water of its own accord. Merely to glimpse these delights is something that makes rowing so very, very worthwhile.

I GET THAT SINKING FEELING

Unlike many of my contemporaries, I have never been in the least interested in preserving medals or cups as mementos of victories. I don't think I have a single medal in my possession. They have all been stolen, lost or carelessly mislaid. Recently, however, I found a plaque with which I was presented when, as Chairman of the Amateur Rowing Association, I attended the European Rowing Championships in Ghent. I was not a little surprised to find that the donor was no less a personage than the Minister of Sanitation of the town from which they "brought the good news". I cannot for the life of me figure out the connection.

Goblets were presented to the winners of the pair-oar race at Henley Regatta, and originally I had eight of them: six of my father's and two of my own. They have all disappeared. Frankly I have no regrets, for they were, without exception, the most hideous cups it has ever been my misfortune to behold. I am glad to say that they have long since been replaced with far more presentable trophies which, had they been given in the years when I was rowing, I should have gone to great lengths to hold on to. The only trophies that I guard with care and handle with affection are the Diamond Sculls Cups won by my father.

If the outward and visible tokens of success are no longer in my possession, I have a treasure chest of happy and ineradicable memories. Amongst so many I have stored a vivid recollection of one grand old man who presented me with the Grand Challenge Cup, together with the appropriate medal, at the Henley Regatta of 1926. At the time of which I am writing he was only one or two years short of his 100th birthday. As he walked to the stand prior to presenting the prizes the band, in honour of his being the oldest Guardsman, broke into a particularly fast rendering of "The British Grenadiers". All his martial ardour came to the fore as, responding to the tune, he made a valiant attempt to quick-march in time to the music. He was, however, persuaded to desist from this attempt; it was feared that the energetic jerks he was injecting into his performance might do him some injury. As he presented me with that noble and gigantic trophy, the Grand Challenge Cup which, such was his frailty, he seemed to have difficulty in supporting, he remarked to me, "Be careful, sir. It's very heavy!"

I quote this episode as I can now boast, quite truthfully, that at the age of twenty-seven I spoke to a man who as a baby had been patted on the head by George IV.

Finally, there are the light-hearted phrases, those little oft-repeated jokes that add to the happiness of the crew. On one occasion, with nerves on edge, we were going down to the start of a race when I quoted a passage from Gilbert and Sullivan's "Yeoman of the Guard". Fairfax in dire trouble, delivers the following lines, "Thou and I have faced the grim old king a dozen times and never has his Majesty come in such goodly fashion." That was remembered and used again and again in successive crews as we went down to face the starter. "Thou and I have faced the grim old king a dozen times and never has his Majesty come to me in such goodly fashion."

A practice course is perhaps the most testing moment. One knows that one is going to row oneself to a pitch of exhaustion bordering on agony without the excitement of the actual race. Could anything be worse? Somehow I fancied that childbirth could be a good deal worse and I expressed my feeling by whispering to Stroke just before the start—"Anyhow I'd sooner row a course than have a baby!" He agreed.

Chapter 15

From Megaphones to Microphones

THERE is no doubt that John Snagge has a great sense of the dramatic. Even the most ordinary piece of information when he reads it is given an undertone of world-shattering importance. Were he asked to recite into the microphone something as innocuous as "Mary had a little lamb" he would undoubtedly endow it with a quality pregnant with surprise and foreboding.

Give him a Boat Race that has devolved into a dreary uneventful procession and he can be relied upon to turn it into the most thrilling Grand National that was ever ridden. This is his great secret, the ability to turn a Boat Race into a steeplechase. The familiar landmarks of the Putney to Mortlake course are treated as though they were jumps. Listening to him, one is almost persuaded that Hammersmith Bridge is Beechers Brook, while Barnes Bridge, by some miraculous tone of voice becomes The Chair.

Listen to him—"Now they're coming up to Hammersmith Bridge. Oxford are just in the lead. Cambridge are spurting. Now they're both under the Bridge and . . . yes . . . yes, they're THROUGH . . . now Oxford . . . etc. etc." In fact the negotiating of Hammersmith Bridge, something well within the capabilities of the worst crew that ever rowed, is transformed into a tremendous feat and made to sound just as exciting as the clearing of Bechers Brook. I take my hat off to him.

This preamble is, I must confess, a prelude to a confession that, backed by the late Sir John Squire, I undertook the first two running commentaries of the Boat Race. This fact has long since been forgotten and perhaps just as well. I wasn't very good at it. Not so bad, however, that they gave me up for good. Some thirty years later, the B.B.C., bless them, invited me to do the commentary on the first TV showing of the Boat Race from a following launch. This was even worse, through no fault of mine. I was gaily prattling into the microphone and watching the TV screen in front of me when a particularly obstreperous wave came on board and my TV packed up. This was about three minutes after the start of the race. The TV pictures continued to go out to the public, but as I hadn't the slightest idea which of the many cameras covering the race was in action at any one moment, the end product could not by any stretch of the imagination be termed synchronized. Personally, I think I put up a very plucky performance. Instead of admitting to a "technical hitch" of the first magnitude, that old conglomeration of darlings known as the B.B.C. made me the scapegoat.

It was through Roger Eckersley that in 1927 I had been given an audition at Savoy Hill to decide whether I should be entrusted with that first wireless commentary of the Boat Race. He and his wife Nancy lived near us at Farnham Common, and we had combined in the production of a series of revues which we had put on annually at Farnham Royal. We had been responsible for a variety of numbers. I thrashed out the lyrics which he set to music. He had a great gift for composing happy and appropriate tunes.

My audition consisted in being asked to read some random prose which was put before me. I presumed that this exercise was to establish the fact that, however much I was lacking in experience, I had at any rate learned to read and been vouchsafed the gift of speech. I was then asked to pretend that an exciting boat race was in progress and comment on what I imagined might be happening. I sensed at once that here was a possible pitfall. In the excitement of the moment there would be a great temptation to break into a torrent of bad language. Any such licence I foresaw would be frowned upon by John Reith, the Director General, if ever my audition should reach his ears. This was just the mistake made, I learned afterwards, by my rivals for the job. By the scrupulous avoidance of swear words and

University Boat Race, 1949, Umpire G. O. Nickalls (with the megaphone in the bows of the right hand launch)

Count F. Van den Heuvel with the author, after a busy day in the Law Courts

The Oxford Connection. Five Oxford rowing blues. Top left, Guy Nickalls, the author's father. Top right, Sir Harcourt Gold, the author's uncle and godfather. Bottom left, R. S. de Havilland, the author's rowing coach and house tutor at Eton. Bottom right, Lord Ampthill, the author's other godfather. Centre, the author. There is no surviving cartoon of Vivian Nickalls, the author's uncle and yet another Oxford rowing blue. All cartoons are by "Spy" (Sir Leslie Ward) except that of the author, which is by Alan Stern. The six recorded an aggregate of 13 Boat Race victories.

FROM MEGAPHONES TO MICROPHONES

the histrionic ability to feign excitement and surprise, I got the job.

My father came along with me to Savoy Hill to see how I made out. I'm sure he did not expect to meet Reith, though in fact he may have felt that he exercised, however slightly, a sort of proprietary right in him. In the early part of the First World War they both lived for a period at Newhaven, U.S.A., occupying respective rooms in the Taft Hotel. I have been given to understand that Reith was engaged on some sort of official liaison job. My father often recalled the remark he made on learning the news that the U.S.A. had entered the war on the side of the Allies, "Good, now I shall be able to wear my kilt."

On this occasion my father was foolhardy enough to bring along a brother of his — a noisy, true blue, reactionary Tory if ever there was one. We were invited to go into the main broadcasting room to see how things happened. It was a large room where everything seemed to be going on at the same time. How different from the galaxy of studios with their solemn, highly efficient and almost ecclesiastical auras of the present day. They were reading the news — "Mr. Ramsay Macdonald is suffering from a slight chill." "Hurrah!" shouted my uncle at the top of his voice. Angry, reproachful hissing sounds followed this unwonted interference and a hundred admonitory fingers pointed to the red light which indicated we were on the air. Not a moment I care to remember.

In the course of the next few days I was told that it was by no means certain that a commentary from a launch in the middle of the river was a possibility. It had never been done before and I mustn't be disappointed if nothing went over at all. I was further told that Jack Squire was to be my number two commentator.

Eventually the day of the race arrived and we found ourselves in the middle of the river in the bows of a launch at Putney. We shared a microphone and Squire got in the first crack. He recalled that amongst the crowd which thronged the bank he had noted a number of religious enthusiasts bearing placards announcing, "There are millions living who will never die!" We had been told, he said, that it was by no means certain our commentary would be heard by the general public and added that were we to carry placards it would be appropriate for them to bear the inscription "There are millions listening who may never hear".

Squire, friendly fellow though he was, was by no means an easy partner in those particular and peculiar circumstances. If, for instance, he thought I was hogging the microphone he would stamp sharply on one of my toes, and as I drew back in agony he would push forward and pour words of wisdom, or otherwise, into the microphone. However, before the finish of the race we had arrived at a tacit and friendly understanding as to our respective functions. As soon as the race was over, Lance Sieveking, who had been in charge of the technicalities of the broadcast, came forward from his seat in the stern of the launch. His face was wreathed in a smile which indicated relief and triumph. It had all been a great success and every word had gone over with the utmost clarity. In fact a message of congratulations to all concerned had already been received from the Director General.

In the years following that first commentary, I gave talks on the radio about boat racing prospects on many occasions. I became rowing correspondent for the *Evening News*, and for a number of years provided the commentary which accompanied the showing of the Boat Race on British Movietone News. John Snagge, moreover, was kind enough to ask me to go along with him and take over the commentary every now and again. I must say I enjoyed that a good deal. Invariably he brought along some gay sparks who could be relied upon to keep one amused. On one such occasion I met Tommy Trinder. A few evenings before I had seen him on television interviewing a certain lady, either in a night club or at some gala or charitable party. The lady in question was well known for her extreme comeliness, her facial beauty being rivalled only by the pulchritude of her bosom. She was wearing a very low-cut dress. In the middle of the interview Tommy Trinder, who was sitting beside

FROM MEGAPHONES TO MICROPHONES

her, announced, "Well, I'd better stand up or I shall be getting rude", and he continued the chat-up from a standing position. He denied that that remark had brought him any adverse criticism. I then asked him if, as the result of his assuming the perpendicular, he received any visual enlightenment. "Yes," he replied, "I was absolutely fascinated. They were obviously lying on shelves."

But all these various engagements were occasions connected only with rowing, and like the clown who yearns to play Hamlet I was longing to extend my activities into other fields. Curiously enough my first release from being a commentator purely on rowing came, not from broadcasting, but from films. I had made the acquaintance of Tony Bushell at the Garrick Club. One day I told him of an occurrence that had happened to me at Henley while I was in the Home Guard. Some time during the darkest days of the war it had been announced that George VI was to inspect the troops in the Western Command. It was further announced that he would stop off at Henley and inspect a platoon of its Home Guard. The unit selected happened to be the one whose duty it was to cover the Henley–Wargrave, Henley–Maidenhead roads, the one in which I was serving as a private. It was felt that some sort of show should be staged for His Majesty and it was arranged that I, with an assistant, would be stationed behind a wall on the Wargrave Road. On a given signal I was to light a Molotov Cocktail and hurl it into the middle of the road. The Molotov Cocktail was simply a glass bottle filled with petrol and the neck plugged with cotton wool. The idea was to light the cotton wool and hurl the bottle at some appropriate target, whereupon a most impressive sheet of flame shuddered impressively some thirty feet into the air. This, we were told, was guaranteed to put paid to any German tank which might come rumbling along the road. What a hope! However, it would have been termed defeatist to breathe a word of doubt as to the efficiency of the weapon with which we had been provided. The King duly arrived. The word was given and I hurled the lighted bottle bang into the middle of the road, where the giant flame soared heavenward as was intended. Elated by my undoubted success I popped my head up from behind the wall, and asking the King and his Staff to stand well back, announced that I was going to throw another one. "For God's sake, don't," implored the King. "We can't afford it." The party then went on their way.

That episode appealed to Tony. It so happened that at that time he was directing the filming of "The Valiant Years". "I'd like to include that," he said. "Meet me down on the Leander raft tomorrow morning and I'll have a film unit come down and we'll re-enact the whole thing. Meanwhile think up all the Home Guard stories you can." That night I started to recall all the ridiculous and idiotic happenings that had occurred. At the appointed time I arrived on the Leander raft and they invited me to start spouting my reminiscences into a microphone—a long, pole-like contraption which one of the team held at arm's length above his head. I went right in and poured forth, as I thought for about ten minutes, when there was a cry of "Break". Imagining that I had perpetrated some unforgivable gaffe, I asked what I had done wrong. "Absolutely nothing," was the reply. "Well, why the break?" I enquired. They reassured me, "Nothing of any importance. It was only that our chap here simply couldn't hold up the microphone any longer. You've been talking for twenty-five minutes. Go on from where you left off." After about another five minutes I came to the end of my thrilling narrative. It was then suggested that I should re-enact and explain the incident of the Molotov Cocktail.

When it was all over a little man summoned me to the seclusion of one of the boathouse doors. Although I am normally conscientious about such matters I took the trouble to ask if their books were scrutinized by the Inland Revenue, and on receiving an assurance to the contrary I accepted some pound notes. By the time the film appeared the actual pith of the story was all that remained. I complained, not very seriously, to Tony Bushell about the brutality of the cutting, only to be met with the reply, "I don't think you have any cause to complain. I timed your bit and found it was a fraction of a second longer than what they allowed Clem Attlee."

Without wishing to disparage the Home Guard or belittle the tremendous energy and enthusiasm they gave to making themselves into irregular soldiers, I sometimes wonder what would have happened in the event of an invasion. For instance, as I understood it one of our main roles would have been to mislead and confuse the invaders to the best of our ability. Amongst other things, signposts were to be uprooted and replaced so that the enemy might find themselves entering High Wycombe under the impression that they had arrived at Oxford. It so happened that there came into my possession some standing instructions issued to the regular and special constabulary. In the event of an invasion their orders were to remain at their posts and to direct the panzer units to their respective destinations. Nothing to do with "misdirecting" them, the word was "directing" them. It seems that the Home Guard and Police objectives were diametrically opposed.

One evening, after an inspiring talk by our battalion commander, questions were invited. I rose from my seat and, after outlining the discrepancy between the orders issued to the respective forces and underlining the confusion that would inevitably result, I asked if in the circumstances the first duty of the Home Guard should not be the annihilation of our own police force. After all, it would greatly simplify our job. A gruesome thing to have to do, no doubt, but regardless of kith and kin our duty was first and foremost to the Home Guard. I was not unduly surprised when I failed to elicit any satisfactory answer.

It was not always easy to devise exercises and miniature battles to keep the men interested and as efficient as possible. My platoon headquarters were in an empty house on the Berkshire side of Henley Bridge. One day in mid-October, to relieve the monotony of parades, I told them that the following week I would put the platoon under the command of my sergeant. His job would be to place the platoon in appropriate positions while I would swim the river from the Oxfordshire bank and endeavour to gain the sanctuary of our H.Q. without being spotted. The H.Q. stood some three hundred yards back from the Berkshire bank and I explained that I would crawl ashore somewhere between two landmarks situated some five hundred yards apart. Late October was the essential time of year for this particular exercise. The men came on to parade when their day's work was over. At that time of year I could rely on the cover of darkness and the temperature of the water would, with any luck, still retain some of its summer warmth. I could rely on not being frozen to death.

Clad in shorts and rowing zephyr I entered the water at a convenient spot upstream of the point on the opposite bank where I had previously noticed a convenient slipway, which would enable me to land without betraying my presence by making the noise inevitably connected with the heaving of oneself up a steep bank. The water was not particularly cold and I swam as silently as possible. About three-quarters of the way across I was fortunate in finding a convoy of swans paddling downstream. They didn't seem to object to my joining them and after all it would take a keen-sighted man to spot a human head masquerading as a cygnet. Conveniently they swam right past the slipway, where I left them; then, swimming in such a way as to require no very great depth of water, I felt my belly scraping along the mud on the bottom. Very gingerly I rose to my feet so that the squelching water running off me made as little noise as possible. No one challenged me. I trotted about a hundred and fifty yards to the Wargrave–Henley road, another three hundred yards and I arrived at our H.Q. I'd got through the lot of them. At that moment our company commander arrived. He questioned my sergeant as to the positioning of his men. Apparently he had placed them at regular intervals on the river bank. This gave the company commander an admirable opportunity of a little homily on the importance of "defence in depth". I hurried home to a hot tub, and my bathroom harboured a distinct aroma of river weed for a week after. Each time I entered it, I recalled Rupert Brooke's lines :

FROM MEGAPHONES TO MICROPHONES

> To sense the meadow sweet and rotten
> Unforgettable, unforgotten river smell...

A few years back John Snagge informed me that I was going to be asked to be the subject of the "Desert Island Disc" programme. I chose my numbers, and when I arrived at Broadcasting House I was met by Roy Plomley, the interviewer of the series, and taken into the record library, surely the most comprehensive collection of discs that has, as yet, been compiled. I had decided to open with what had become the signature tune of that great pianist Myra Hess—"Jesu, joy of man's desiring". I chose one from one of the five renderings offered to me. There followed a number beautifully sung by Helga Mott, a woman whom I have adored ever since the day when first I met her. It was the "Kleiner Hotel". During the most depressing days of the war, she had sung this and other Viennese waltzes to the huge delight of many thousands of people. The fact that she has a goodly drop of Viennese blood in her veins proved a distinct advantage.

As to the object I would most dearly desire to have with me on a Desert Island, I chose Rembrandt's portrait of his son Titus—a magnificent picture which had recently changed hands at Christie's for an all time record sum of £780,000. A kind lady from Richmond presented me with a copy she had made of the original; a gift which I greatly treasure.

There was one little incident connected with the recording of this programme which appealed to me. Towards the end of the session a friend of mine arrived at the studio and was immediately ushered in to the recording room where Monica Chapman was in charge. She was eventually forced to ring up and ask for an extension of time. Forgetting that I had a friend in the room she rang up and explained her dilemma. "I'm awfully sorry, darling, to have to ask for an extension, but you must understand I have an oldie here who simply will go on." How right she was. I know I was over-garrulous but that is liable to happen with me when I am thoroughly enjoying myself.

A RAINBOW IN THE SKY

A year or so later, John Garton, the Chairman of the Committee of Management of Henley Regatta suggested that I should write an article or do a broadcast which, however slightly, should include a reference to the fact that there was such an event as Henley Regatta. I appealed to John Snagge for help. He suggested I get in touch with Joanna Scott-Moncrieff of the B.B.C. I did so and after perusing an article of mine which had been turned down by two journals she started right away to suggest how it might be adapted for inclusion in a series of programmes for which she was responsible entitled "Pause for Thought". She told me that the length of time at my disposal would involve about seven hundred and fifty words, suggesting that the title should be "Endeavour" and that this talk should embrace endeavour as it applied to rowing and painting.

Eventually I recorded it and over it went, and it made me very happy when a few weeks later she wrote and asked whether I would do another talk. At her instigation, I did four in all. After the first one there was scarcely a reference to rowing. This pleased me hugely. She had aided and abetted my yearnings to break through the rowing barrier.

Chapter 16

All At Sea

I AM no sailor. I speak from experience. I am no sooner on board a yacht than a host of inanimate objects attack me with venom. They band together to make my voyage one of utter misery. If it isn't a boom practising its well-known decapitation act, then it's a cleat determined to enter my body in the most painful possible way or an overexcited rope lashing me across the face. A ten-ton cutter in the hands of an inexperienced skipper is the most ingenious torture chamber yet devised.

One wonderful summer after some success at Henley Regatta, my dear old friend Luke (R. S. C. Lucas) was kind enough to ask me as a guest aboard his recently acquired vessel. The idea was that we should meet at Hamble, make our way across the Solent, enjoy some of the delights of Cowes Week, and then sail west along the south coast and eventually meet up with my family who were holidaying at Salcombe. It sounded ideal, and I felt it would come as a welcome relief from the violent exercise which had been our lot since the beginning of the year.

We were to be accompanied by an ancient mariner, who I gathered would help with the navigation. My first sight of our ten-ton boat aroused my suspicions. It was a rough little number, not at all the spick-and-span swan-like apparition I had imagined. It must surely have been launched in the last decade of the nineteenth century. But however old, it cannot have been older than our ancient mariner, who greeted me as I stepped on board. His aspect gave me no sort of confidence in his chances of survival as far as Salcombe. Tentatively I enquired as to his qualifications. "Oh," replied Luke with a somewhat forced nonchalance. "He's a local chap I picked up. He's very good at working a fire engine." I let it rest at that; to delve further into his abilities might have seemed a trifle impolite. I sent up a silent prayer that his dexterity in the manipulation of fire engines would never be put to the test. At the same time the first clouds of disillusionment began to steal over my horizon.

As we set sail Luke started browsing over some vastly important-looking charts. He then went through the motions of taking various bearings. "I say, old boy," he announced quite cheerfully. "We seem to be in the middle of a minefield." (Relics, I presumed, of the First World War that had not as yet been gelded.) I consoled myself with the thought that if in fact he had made some terrible error it would be most unlikely that we should ever know anything about it.

It was dusk when we glided into Cowes harbour, which none of us had previously entered. Hundreds of craft of every description rode peacefully at anchor. We chose a gap in their serried ranks, edged our way into position and dropped anchor. Just as we were congratulating ourselves on the deftness of this manœuvre, we discovered that the way on our boat had carried us well beyond the anchorage we had intended to occupy and that we had come to rest in mid-channel between two lines of craft. Somehow or other we edged our way back into line and prepared for a peaceful night.

We were unduly optimistic. Within minutes an ominous grating sound combined with the fact that we were on the move again suggested we were dragging our anchor. Out of all those hundreds of boats we were the only one who failed to remain fast and secure. "I see what it is," cried Luke triumphantly. "We are the only one who is not anchored fore and aft. We must put out another anchor." But first and foremost we had to regain our original position and by then the tide was running quite fast. "Just a question of starting our auxiliary engine," announced Luke. This in itself was a feat of some magnitude. The starting handle was missing, and the only way to coax the engine into action was to grasp the fly-wheel and revolve it with sufficient power to make the engine start. I was sent forward to weigh anchor, and with superhuman efforts Luke started the auxiliary. (This manœuvre was beset with danger. Should the boat roll ever so slightly the fly-wheel contacted the bilge water and sent sheets of spray hurtling all over the cabin.) On this occasion nothing untoward occurred. Our hopes rose — but only for a moment. The engine spluttering to a standstill was the signal for me to pay out anchor again. This happened three or four times until at last the engine fired with greater confidence. It was at this moment we found to our horror that the propulsive powers of the engine were insufficient to overcome the run of the tide and that instead of making progress we continued to be swept backwards, although at a slower speed. What was our next move? The wind was in the right direction and we felt that the engine, aided by sail-power, might overcome the strength of the tide. Much to our relief we were proved right. Had anyone been around, which thank God they were not, our appearance must have struck a somewhat bizarre note. With the mainsail hoisted and engine revving, we advanced gradually on to our objective at a steady half knot.

At last we were in position with our main anchor on the bottom. Luke put the kedge into our dinghy and paddled aft a suitable distance prior to casting it overboard. Then some quite inexplicable things happened. The kedge became attached to various encumbrances on the sea bed. At one moment he seemed to be hauling on board a chain, each link of which I would estimate measured some nine or ten inches, and then with herculean strength he proceeded to pass the stern of our boat underneath this mighty chain, which surely would have held fast a man-o-war had it been put to the test. The precise function of this chain was never revealed. By the number of barnacles and the amount of seaweed it had gathered to it, it seemed to have been lying on the sea bed for some considerable time. Meanwhile our ancient fire-fighting mariner took no very active part in the proceedings. Every now and then he was heard to mutter a pious hope to the effect that he'd soon get the hang of it.

A RAINBOW IN THE SKY

At last we appeared to be stationary, anchored fore and aft in the approved style. We breathed a sigh of intense relief, and prepared to turn in. As it turned out, we were once again unduly optimistic. For some unaccountable reason our boat started to swing and before we could do anything about it our bowsprit had crashed through the glass windows of the most immaculate-looking motor launch in the harbour. We held our breath; surely the tinkling of shattered glass would be followed by some sort of voluble protest? To our amazement nothing happened. Everyone seemed to have gone ashore for the night and we continued to drift about more or less out of control until we bumped into a recently converted M.L., which happened to be occupied. The party on board were kindness itself. Luke explained our predicament and suggested apologetically that we should be less of a nuisance if they could make us fast to their magnificent launch. A word from the owner and a boarding party leapt down on to our deck and in true seamanlike fashion made us fast alongside them. At last we were able to turn in and get some rest, though not for as long as we had hoped. At about 5 a.m. Luke let forth a roar of apprehension. We were aground and heeling over on our side. Luckily he said he knew what to do. From amongst his clutter of equipment he produced some iron rods which if fixed in the proper position would, so he assured me, prevent our boat heeling right over on its side. He was right. By some miracle they seemed to prevent us assuming a more perilous angle, Meanwhile we sat, wet and cold, on the edge of our deck and waited in misery until the tide turned and we were once more on an even keel. We went below to the shelter of the cabin. But afloat, things were astir. A party boarded the launch which the previous evening had received the unwelcome attentions of our bowsprit. We peered apprehensively through our portholes. "Hullo, hullo," we heard a voice complaining. "There's been dirty work going on here last night." I wasn't in charge, but there was no doubt in my mind that we should come clean. In horror we watched them as they weighed anchor. Would our anchor be entangled with theirs and thereby reveal us as the culprits? As it was they completed their task without any trace of our anchor surfacing simultaneously.

Meanwhile it had occurred to us that if we tidied ourselves up a bit we might be invited on board the splendid M.L., which we had learned from one of the crew was the property of Sir Howard Frank. We dived for our luggage and donned our white flannel trousers which we had brought for just this sort of occasion. We put on clean shirts and thought that our Leander ties might help matters. It worked. We strolled up and down our deck with an absent-minded air, when Howard Frank shouted across to us that they were going out to watch the six-metre racing, and would we care to join them and stay on board for lunch? Needless to say we jumped at the opportunity, and were straightway enjoying a sense of utter luxury which contrasted strangely with the stresses and strains of the last twenty-four hours. We thanked Howard Frank for this great kindness, though I don't think he ever realized the extent of our gratitude. We had enjoyed a most wonderful day. He was kind enough to afford us another carefree night made fast to his sumptuous and sheltering M.L. Cowes week was now over and we went on our respective ways, never to meet again.

Luke decided that Yarmouth (Isle of Wight) was our next port of call; reckoning that by spending the night there and by making an early start we should reach Weymouth on the following day. We were grateful that, compared to Cowes, Yarmouth harbour was comparatively empty. Our anchor continued to drag and by the morning we had become well-acquainted with the geography of the harbour. The next morning a favourable tide carried us out past the Needles. It was an uneventful day. We fried some sausages for lunch. Even the simplest culinary manœuvre could be accomplished only by sitting on the lavatory seat and stretching in cramped surroundings towards an ancient gas stove. Late that evening the study of yet another sailing manual, which suggested that by aligning a cliff-hanging church with a prominent telegraph pole, we should make a successful and trouble-free entrance to Weymouth harbour proved, by some astonishing coincidence, to be entirely correct.

Our main problem the following day was to avoid being caught in the tide race off Portland Bill. The maritime guide books we had with us advised that to avoid the tide race we should keep as close as possible to the mainland. As if to emphasize this point it was suggested that we should feel that by hurling a biscuit towards the shore it would fall on dry land. Further study of our sailing manual seemed to indicate that the author was particularly keen on the hurling of a random biscuit as a criterion of distances.

As we approached the tide race, whose turbulence was clearly visible ahead of us, Luke decided that he was suffering from constipation and that his only chance of survival was to lie down in his bunk. It was an inappropriate moment for such a decision. The ancient mariner took the helm and it was obvious that he was setting his course much too far from the shore. In fact he was making straight for the tide race. I pointed this out to him at five-minute intervals, only to be met by a stubborn disregard of the obvious. "I was always a deep sea sailor, I was," he proclaimed as though that ended the argument once and for all. Then, as though to give me confidence, he added that his nephew was in the Merchant Navy and that he was in possession of charts which told one how to get to Brazil. He wished he had them with him. Somehow he seemed to think that these charts would soon put a stop to all my foolish shore-hugging chatter. He cast a pitying glance in my direction. It was quite obvious that my failure immediately to appreciate the connection proved conclusively that I was a half-wit. Suddenly the tide race had us in its grip. Like a matchstick caught in a whirlpool the boat turned round three times as though we were a piece of flotsam about to be sucked down a plughole. This thoroughly frightened the ancient mariner, who shouted to Luke in a frenzy of apprehension: "Come on up, sir. It's all rot. We must 'ave all 'ands on deck. She's taken a round robin out of me — she 'as." Very unwillingly, and still protesting at the inconvenience of his constipation, Luke stumbled up on deck.

At that moment a favourable gust of wind aided by a wonderful piece of luck saved us from our somewhat terrifying predicament and all was well again.

We sailed in a westerly direction, and as the afternoon wore on it became fairly obvious that we were unlikely to make landfall that night. We had only the vaguest idea of where we were, and as dusk came the wind rose and it was clear that we were in for a stormy night. At all costs we must keep well clear of the shore. The wind was northerly, and we decided that our best plan would be to run before the wind out into the Channel. About midnight it was obvious by the lights of various vessels that we were approaching the line of Channel shipping. Instead of port and starboard lights slung in the appropriate positions we had a miserable lantern surrounded by coloured glass. Half the surrounding glass was the red port light and half the green starboard light. By revolving this cylinder of glass we could show a port or starboard light as we chose. For minutes on end I would hold the port light on our port side and then by revolving the glass until we were showing a green light we held it out to starboard. I guessed it to be a matter of pure chance whether any other shipping would even see the light. The wind had risen to gale force and the possibility of colliding with some vessel that would smash us to pieces seemed imminent. We had mighty little control had things gone wrong. More by luck than good judgement we avoided being shipwrecked and careered wildly through the oncoming boats. We were shipping a good deal of water and it was coming aboard green. We were towing our dinghy, which was filling fast. Luke asked me to go forward and release a loose rope which had entwined itself round the tin stovepipe emanating from the galley. For some unknown reason I had been expecting a quiet night and was clad only in pyjamas. I was soaked to the skin, very cold, and experiencing the greatest difficulty in maintaining a hold on the boat. Frankly I was terrified. Just as I was returning aft a loud ping announced the fact that a rope had given up the ghost. "It's gone! It's gone!" cried Luke. "What's gone?" I asked. "The rope towing the dinghy. We've lost our dinghy. We shall never see it again!" After what seemed an interminable time the conditions became calmer, and a glow from the east announced sunrise. Thank God! What a nightmare! Somehow we had survived. Luke remained calm. "By sailing due west, we should strike Salcombe," he announced. "No, thank you!" I retorted. "Let's sail north and strike England." He saw my point. Early that afternoon we entered Brixham harbour, and running up towards a buoy dislodged a superior-looking seagull, and hanging on to the buoy with our boathook, we shouted to the Harbour Master, "Would he come and rescue us? We had lost our dinghy." "I wonder some of you amateurs don't get drowned — I do," he said. I left Luke the next morning. He said he would join me at Salcombe when he had done a bit of refitting. He never did.

I have cause to remember that holiday at Salcombe for one particular incident. One morning we found the town plastered with placards announcing that a grand regatta would take place in a few days' time. The events included not only sailing but swimming races of various distances. By way of variety there was a race in which it was incumbent on the swimmers to push a barrel in front of them as they swam. I had never thought of doing that but I felt it might be an amusing experience. Feeling that I might as well make an afternoon of it whilst I was about it, I entered also for the quarter mile and two hundred yard races as well — three events in all. As it turned out I won one of the races and was second in the other two.

At seven o'clock we were invited to appear at the Town Hall to receive our prizes, which I imagined would be some form of cup or medal, appropriate to the occasion. My name was called, I advanced to receive my award and was somewhat astonished to have fifty-five shillings pressed into my hand. Now in rowing, the rules defining amateurism are very strict. Compete for a money prize and forthwith you become a professional. This rule does not apply to rowing only. To accept a money prize in any other sport, or to have competed against those who had competed for money, debars you from rowing as an amateur. I felt it would be priggish in the extreme to have refused their fifty-five shillings. I accepted it and kept mum. I suppose by making a clean breast of the whole affair I should have received absolution and a formal reinstatement as an amateur. Somehow or other I didn't bother. I just let it slide and went on to enjoy another ten years of amateur rowing, though from a strictly technical viewpoint I was now undoubtedly a professional.

Chapter 17

"Please to Stop the Shooting"

In 1952 I was elected Chairman of the Amateur Rowing Association, thereby succeeding my uncle, Sir Harcourt Gold. It is in no spirit of criticism that I record that, in spite of all the forward-looking and imaginative activities in which he engaged on behalf of rowing he, like the great majority of his contemporaries, had no very great love for its international aspects. It is true that under him this country became a member of the Fédération Internationale Société d'Aviron, invariably referred to as F.I.S.A., yet when it became a question of representation at the European Championships I was, almost invariably, asked to deputize for him. It did not take any particular foresight on my part to realize that the ambition of the majority of young men, active in rowing at that time, was to succeed internationally and to set their sights beyond the somewhat restricted competition to be found in this country.

It was my experience of rowing abroad which prompted Harold Rickett to ask me to make a date with the representatives of Soviet rowing who had just taken up residence in Henley before their first appearance at the Regatta in 1954. In short I was to tell them the sort of things to expect, and explain how and why our rules differed in a few minor details from the F.I.S.A. rules to which they had been accustomed. I went up to their training quarters on the outskirts of Henley to try, through an interpreter, to carry out my mission.

After the preliminary introductions they started firing questions at me. It was obvious from the beginning that they harboured the deepest suspicions of our honesty. They seemed convinced that by hook or by crook (they seemed to

"PLEASE TO STOP THE SHOOTING"

think it would be the latter) we should deny them the victory they deserved.

Their first question was to ask whether they could have three representatives aligned with the finishing post. I told them in the gentlest possible way that not only would they have no representatives at the finishing post but it was most unlikely that they would have any representatives within fifty yards of it. I noted that several of them exchanged glances as much as to say "I told you so". I went on to assure them that we didn't cheat and that it would be most unlikely that for the past sixty years crews from America would have continued to compete again and again had we been in the habit of doing so.

My questioners were sitting around me in a ring. My eye had been caught by a particularly fine-looking specimen, bigger and bonnier than the rest. I was just thinking what an asset he would be in any crew when I suddenly realized that "he" was a "she". It was in fact the woman doctor. She was just about to ask the interpreter a question when something went off with a terrifying report. They all jumped in astonishment and I, indicating that there was no cause for alarm, waited for the next question. The doctor wanted to know if she could pitch a first-aid tent in the Stewards Enclosure so that at any moment she could spring from her lair, get in a dinghy, and row out and succour any Soviet oarsman whose exertions had caused his collapse. I explained that there would be a number of highly qualified medical men present whom we kept on hand against just such an emergency. There was another deafening report and this time I realized that the perpetrators of this so-called joke were an English crew. Their headquarters were next door and to endear themselves to their Russian rivals they were lobbing squibs over the dividing walls. Bloody fools!

"Mr. Neekalls (as they called me), why are not your rules exactly the same as those laid down by F.I.S.A.?" To have entered into details regarding the niceties of our rulings and the reasons for them would have taken all night. A short cut had to be found. "I understand that in the Soviet Union you have been responsible for many wonderful inventions," I ventured. "Yes, yes, yes." They took my point exactly. I continued, "And when you have invented something, you don't allow other people to alter it or mess about with it." "No, no, no, Mr. Neekalls," they all agreed. "Well," I continued "We invented rowing as a sport and, having invented it, we don't let other people mess about with it. You understand?" This was no answer at all—just a piece of sheer nonsense blurted out on the spur of the moment. However, they seemed perfectly satisfied. In fact they seemed to accept it with a certain awe as though there was no gainsaying the weight of my logic.

After a few other questions they asked me to stay and have some supper with them, but could they ask one favour? "Would Mr. Neekalls, please, stop the shooting." I found this a very reasonable request and said I would do what I could. I sometimes wonder who they thought were being shot. Perhaps some of our less successful oarsmen whose performance merited extreme measures. The next day, after I had delivered a few well-chosen words to the culprits, there was no more "shooting".

At dinner we drank vodka and scraped caviare from little glass jars. One of the courses consisted of poached eggs. To say they were cold would be an understatement. They were straight out of the ice-box and I thought them absolutely revolting. On the other hand, the Russians seemed to relish them.

Towards the end of dinner our vodka intake quickened, and then

"Is Mr. Neekalls married?" — "Yes".
"As 'e any children?" — "No".
"Are 'is parents alive" — "No".

Having thus mutually agreed on the next step, with one accord and upraised glasses it was: "And so we drink to Mrs. Neekalls!"

And then, between quickfire gulps of vodka, the interpreter said, "Mr. Neekalls, they say as our guest you should

"PLEASE TO STOP THE SHOOTING"

have double vodka." I replied, "On the contrary you should have double vodka," and pointed to the interpreter. My remark was duly translated to them. "They ask why, Mr. Neekalls, should I have double vodka." "Because you've done double the talking." This rather weak sally absolutely slayed them. They bellowed with uncontrollable laughter. They rocked to and fro, holding their sides in a Falstaffian manner. "Oh, Mr. Neekalls, you are so vonny." It was as if no one ever before had said anything quite so intoxicatingly witty.

The draw to decide who should row against whom, and on what station, is decided by putting paper slips, bearing the names of the crews, into the Grand Challenge Cup and drawing them out one by one. This ceremony takes place in public at the Henley Town Hall on the Saturday prior to the Regatta.

It was generally acknowledged that the eventual winner of the Grand Challenge Cup lay between two crews — the Soviet and some other crew from overseas whose practice performances had made a great impression. It so happened that the draw that particular year ordained quite by chance that these two crews could not meet each other until the final. In fact they were on opposite sides of the draw. Just a matter of luck; yet nothing would persuade the Russians that, by some elaborate piece of chicanery, the draw had not been rigged. After the draw they approached the Chairman with "Meester Rickett, we know you feex the draw but we do not zee 'ow you do it." Nothing, in fact, would persuade them otherwise.

On the Sunday morning prior to the opening of the Regatta there is an Oarsmen's Service in St. Mary's Parish Church, close by Henley Bridge. The Russians were anxious to do the right thing. Afterwards their impressions of the service were given to the Press. "We liked the way all the English oarsmen sang the hymns. The Minister was not so good. Anyhow, how can one go to church if one studies science?"

At the Regatta a certain number of guests are taken on the Umpire's launch, which follows the race. This privilege carried with it the obvious proviso that no one on board is allowed to communicate by speech or by signs with either of the racing crews—the Umpire's launch, so to speak, being neutral territory. It so happened that I umpired the race in which the Soviet pair-oar were engaged. They won their race, and again I found myself umpiring their race on the following day. In the meantime I had been informed that one of the Russian coaches sitting in the bows of the launch had been seen surreptitiously signalling to his crew during the race. He had been, in fact, helping them with their steering—a heinous offence. His object would be to keep them straight on course and prevent them colliding with the floating wooden booms or buoys which line the course. Before their next race I sat a friend of mine next to the Russian in question, telling him to keep a sharp look-out and to prevent the Russian giving any signals to his crew. It transpired that almost immediately signals started passing and that my watchful friend struck the Russian a violent blow on the arm. He got the message, which I thought I would emphasize myself. When the Soviet pair-oar had won the race, I went to a lot of trouble to shake hands with and congratulate all the other Russians on the launch excepting the offender. He noticed this and offered his hand, which I refused to shake. I happen to be one of those fools who believe that even if you don't speak the language, your meaning will get through if you speak your own tongue sufficiently slowly and with the correct emphasis and intonation. On this occasion, instead of shaking hands, I pointed at him and said very deliberately "YOU MUST LEARN NOT TO CHEAT AT GAMES". "But, Mr. Neekalls," he pleaded, "our men did not know the course." As the course happens to be dead straight, there could never have been any question of their "knowing" it. It was just a question of their steering straight.

On one occasion a crew from the Soviet Union went out of their water to such an extent that they were in danger of colliding with their opponents. I warned them that they were out of their water and they changed course and about a minute later collided with the boom, and lost the race. On

"PLEASE TO STOP THE SHOOTING"

that occasion they accused me of deliberately steering them into the boom.

At Henley, oarsmen, on occasions, enter for more than one event on the same day. In those circumstances, in order to give competitors as much time as possible between races, we put their number one event early in the programme and their second event as late as possible. Now Soviet oarsmen are inclined to have their lunch at three o'clock in the afternoon. One day, owing to other oarsmen having two races, they were put down to row at three. This didn't suit them and they started arguing the toss. When they realized that we were not going to give way they said, through their interpreter, that in their opinion ours was "a bloody rotten regatta" to which Harold Rickett, with admirable restraint, said they were perfectly entitled to express their opinion of the Regatta, but they would row at three or not at all. At this point they capitulated.

One year their boats failed to arrive at Henley. They were held up by a dock strike. David Williams, at that time Secretary of the Regatta, worked round the clock to get their boats released, but to no avail. Eventually the Russians wrote a note saying that as Mr. Williams wouldn't let them have their boats they withdrew from all events. We breathed a sigh of relief when the boats eventually arrived in the nick of time.

I recall these early difficulties only so that I can emphasize that they have been long since swept into the limbo of forgotten things. All their suspicions are now finally allayed. There is complete accord, and a satisfying rapprochement has developed between us. They are very welcome at Henley whenever they like to come. Let's hope it will be frequently.

Just one more episode I have always enjoyed. The Russian delegate at one of the European Championships informed me that he had written a book on rowing and would like to present me with a copy. Now it so happened that some thirty years before I, together with Dr. Pat Mallam, had, at the behest of Pitmans, written a book on rowing. The Russian handed over the book he had written and signed his name on the cover. I thanked him profusely and handed the book to Freddie Page, the Secretary of the Amateur Rowing Association, who happened to be able to read Russian. After reading a few pages Freddie, with a broad smile, exclaimed, "But this is your book word for word!" He turned a few more pages and there were the self-same illustrations as I had used. I'm sure my dear Russian friend was completely unaware that I was the victim of his plagiarism, and I, for once, kept my mouth shut.

Chapter 18

Wigs, Gowns and Tow-ropes

I NEVER studied the law nor have I ever been involved in legal cases of the least importance. I have however entered the law courts arrayed as a junior; an experience which must be almost unique in the annals of jurisprudence.

Although it all happened many years ago I think it wise to withhold the name of the perpetrator of this particular prank, who happened to be an old friend of mine. It so happened that I had proposed him for membership of the Garrick Club, and having been seconded by a mutual friend he was duly elected. By way of thanks he thought he would mark the occasion by standing his proposer and seconder a lunch at the Club. I remember it well, one of those carefree luncheons where everything went right from the start. The newly elected member was determined to show his gratitude and with the help of copious draughts of wine the party became positively hilarious. Just as we were enjoying our second glass of port, the new member announced, "I tell you what we'll do now. I'll take you back to my chambers, dress you up as juniors and then we'll do a round of the courts." To us in our devil-may-care post-prandial mood, it sounded one of the merriest pranks ever suggested. We accepted with alacrity. Off we went to our host's chambers. There we giggled helplessly as we fitted our wigs, adjusted our neckwear and donned our gowns. Finally, to complete the picture, some ancient deeds were tied up with pink tape and thrust into our hands. Off the three of us set for the law courts, with this final admonition: "By the way, make a great point of being polite to policemen. We always are."

We entered a court, apparently at random. Our host had told us that we should be invited to occupy one of the benches at the back of the court, which seemed to be reserved for juniors whose legal duties had given them sufficient respite to listen to cases far removed from their own particular orbit.

We asked some of the occupants of the rear benches to move down so that we could be seated alongside them. Having made ourselves comfortable I began to pick up the threads of the case that was being heard. I glanced up and to my great surprise discovered that the case was being heard before the Lord Chief Justice — Lord Goddard. At that time I was living in Henley and Lord Goddard was staying not far away. In the course of commuting we had been introduced and quite often found ourselves in the same carriage. It never occurred to me that he would remember me. Just as I was getting thoroughly interested in the case I noticed our host signalling with such violence that it left no doubt in our minds that he wished us to leave the court immediately. We scrambled out, at great inconvenience to our immediate neighbours. "What's wrong?" we enquired when we got out into the passage. "I was watching Goddard," he explained. "He spotted Gully and I saw him pondering with a wrinkled brow. Somehow or other it had never occurred to him that Gully was connected with the law." How right he was! We paid cursory visits to one or two other courts, and having decided that we had squeezed the last drop of fun from our calls made our way into the Strand and walked in the direction of Charing Cross. There was at that time a photographer there who specialized in passport work, and we felt we would like to have a permanent record of our ludicrous escapade. I'm bound to say we were delighted with the result.

I was recalling the episode to some friends in The Garrick the following day and the question immediately arose as to what penalty, if any, would be imposed on the culprit had our improper conduct been revealed. "There's Pat over there," said one of them. "Let's ask him." As the late Sir Patrick Hastings passed our table on his way to pay his bill, the problem was put to him. "It's contempt of court," he answered abruptly. "Maybe," said his questioner, "but what happens if the plot is discovered?" "It's contempt of court," repeated Pat Hastings and went on his way. The general opinion seemed to be that the perpetrator had run the risk of being struck off. I would dearly love to reveal his name, but it so happens that he is still practising, and though I think it most unlikely that any action would be taken after such a length of time, in fairness to him I must resist the temptation. After all, he had provided us with a whole heap of good, clean fun. Bless him!

I was once called upon to serve on a grand jury. In fact it must have been one of the last grand juries. I seem to remember that, soon after, this seemingly cumbersome piece of legal machinery was abolished. But I was called for ordinary jury service on various occasions. I remember a certain case which promised to be a lively affair, but never materialized. It was brought against John Christie of Glyndebourne fame. When first I knew him he was a science master at Eton, but at a later date, in addition to having founded and controlled Glyndebourne, he had become the proprietor of an organ-manufacturing company. I suppose in the course of a year there is no very big demand for organs. It follows therefore that when the purchase of a new organ is mooted the competition to win the order is fairly keen. A certain company had sent out a brochure giving details of the range of organs they had sold, which appeared to have given great satisfaction. A few days later a representative of John Christie's firm called on a parson who had been made responsible for the purchase of a new organ. During the course of the interview this representative noted the brochure of the rival firm lying on a table. This was altogether too much of a temptation for the poor man. We were told that irrefutable evidence would be called to the effect that, pointing to the brochure, he had said, "I see you have heard from that firm. I can tell you straightaway that you'll get a noise from their organ all right, but it won't be music!" In the circumstances I was not very surprised to learn that, after a short discussion, the case had been settled out of court.

On another occasion I was on a motoring case before

Lord Chief Justice Hewart. The jury were issued with plans showing where the accident had taken place. It didn't take us very long to find that half the jury had been issued with one plan and the other half with a totally different plan. "Please, m'lud, we haven't all got the same plan." "Haven't you?" retorted Hewart. "That's quite usual," and proceeded to sort the matter out.

By far the most entertaining judge I ever heard was Rigby Swift, whose wit and repartee had become a legend in his lifetime. With his cherubic face and clipped Liverpool accent it was sheer joy to see him at work. He had no use for a counsel who was inclined to be long-winded. In fact when he got bored he would kick the desk in front of him. This was a sure sign that his patience was running out. On one occasion a junior was arguing at some length on behalf of his client. Rigby Swift was showing ominous signs of boredom, to such an extent that the leader passed a note to his junior which read—"For God's sake sit down. The old so & so's with us." Swift spotted the note as it passed from hand to hand. "Someone has passed a piece of paper in court. Give me that piece of paper." Counsel, terrified that his reading of the message might possibly prejudice his case, did his best. "M'lud," he said. "I'm sure it wouldn't interest you. It's a purely personal matter between m'learned friend and me." "Give me that piece of paper," repeated Swift. "But, m'lud...." "Give me that piece of paper." Finally it was passed up to Swift. The court waited in silent trepidation whilst he read it. "Have you read this piece of paper?" demanded Swift to the junior. "Yes, m'lud, but..." "Well, read it again," Swift interrupted him. He'd made his point.

The case at which I was present concerned a professional man who walked between two moving cars, one of which was on tow. He had tripped over the tow-rope, fallen heavily, and broken various bones in his arm. He was now suing the tow-rope owner for damages. Some time was taken establishing the fact that the tow-rope had no sort of distinguishing mark to draw attention to the fact that the two vehicles were in any way connected. It was hardly surprising that the plaintiff came a cropper. So serious was his accident, his counsel informed the court, that his client's arm had been shortened by no less than three inches. A handicap which was bound to affect his golf for the remainder of his days. A minute later, however, his Counsel informed us that "three inches" was a slip of the tongue. It should have been three-quarters of an inch. "There is a difference," remarked Rigby Swift drily.

It so happened that Reggie Manningham-Buller, afterwards to become Lord Chancellor and assume the title of Lord Dilhorne was appearing for the defendant. I had known him for many a long year and for some reason he laboured under an illusion that "I'd always been against him" or so he informed me after the case. In fact to such an extent had this opinion become a fixation that as soon as he had seen that I was on the jury he had sent a note to Rigby Swift which read, "Unfortunately I have a friend on the jury. Will you dismiss it and call another." Swift scribbled a note and sent it back to him. "I've often had friends on the jury and I've had to put up with it. So will you."

Reggie Manningham-Buller argued that an exactly parallel case had come before Swift only the previous year. A man had stepped out of a train, assuming that he would be alighting on a platform. As it happened there was no platform there. He had injured himself and Swift had held him negligent and the railway company in no way to blame. Without a pause Swift came back with this very logical reply—"Everybody knows that when you get out of a train, you've got to look to see if there's a platform. But everybody doesn't know that when you walk between two cars you've got to look to see if there's a tow-rope." In his summing up, he told us that if we found for the claimant he would remind us that he was entitled to monetary recompense for every moment of pain he had suffered. "As regards the amount of that recompense, I can give you no sort of guidance." He continued, "You are not allowed to say that the defendant is a small garage proprietor who cannot afford to pay. That doesn't enter into it. And I would remind you that it's just as painful to be run over by a Morris as a

A RAINBOW IN THE SKY

Rolls-Royce." As we stepped down from the jury box I tripped and fell headlong. This was too great a temptation for Rigby Swift. "Juror!" he exclaimed, "that's not my tow-rope." We found for the claimant. We assessed the value of his pain at £400.

A few months later I met Reggie again. "As soon as I saw you on the jury I knew you would be against me," he remarked. "You drove my poor little client into bankruptcy." It was obvious that nothing would rid him of that overriding impression. I was in fact very sorry for his client. But after all, I was only doing what I believed to be right.

Chapter 19

A Peep Behind the "Iron Curtain"

In the years immediately following the Second World War, F.I.S.A.'s (Fédération Internationale Société d'Aviron), declared policy was to turn its back on both East and West Germany. At a later date it agreed to accept delegations from both sides of the Iron Curtain providing that the two entities combined to make one German team. It was left to their representatives to arrange trial races in order to decide which of the two camps would have the honour of representing Germany in any given event.

As the years went by it was noticed that the German team was invariably drawn from West Germany. Was East Germany incapable of providing crews of sufficient calibre? Questioned on this point, it soon became clear that East was East and West was West and never the twain would meet. Each declared that they had done their best, but whenever the question of trial races was mooted, neither side could get an answer to their letters regarding the time and place of any trial races. It should be understood that in so far as the F.I.S.A. was concerned, politics figured prominently in their deliberations, so that when it came to a vote the Iron Curtain countries voted one way and the West the other.

There came a moment when it seemed to me that it was high time that both West and East Germany should each be allowed to enter teams, and I expressed this opinion at the annual F.I.S.A. conference. I said that it was nonsense to keep an embargo on a two-team Germany. I suggested that the eventual reunification of Germany had best be forgotten, we were dealing with things as they were not as some of us would like them to be. I went further. I ventured that the only cause for which the Soviet would go to war would be to prevent any such reunification. I added, "Should it ever get as far as that, and let's pray to God that it doesn't, then it would be extremely unlikely that any of us present would survive to continue this particular argument. Let us therefore be realists and deal with things as they are. There should be two teams for two Germanys."

My motion was lost. Great Britain, for the first time in its history, voted with the Communist bloc. The whole question came up for debate again the following year, and again we were defeated. At our third attempt we were told that, if we were patient, then what we were seeking might come to pass. I gathered that what was really happening was that the President of the F.I.S.A. was waiting for the International Olympic Council to make up its mind on this question as it applied to other sports. I was disappointed. I had always felt that the F.I.S.A. should lead rather than follow the I.O.C., for whom, at that period in its history, I had no very high regard.

At the close of the meeting in which I had originally pleaded for a realistic approach to this problem I was surrounded by a congratulatory bevy of Communists, who were frankly amazed at the view I had taken. Whether or not they thought that I had at last mended my ways and toed the party line I didn't know. I do know that at that particular moment they seemed to regard me as some sort of Messiah, who would put all injustices to rights. Eventually, when a two-team Germany had become a fact, I received an invitation to visit East Germany and to attend one of their regattas, all expenses, including air fares, to be paid by them. I jumped at the opportunity. I had motored through East Germany a few years previously on my way to some Rowing Championships in Poland, and on one occasion I had driven from its Western Sector into East Berlin having obtained the necessary passes. I remember our chauffeur on that occasion would not deviate from the main street which led through the Eastern precincts of the city. When we re-entered West Berlin through the Brandenburg Gate, I noticed that his face was pale and glistened with sweat.

A PEEP BEHIND THE "IRON CURTAIN"

He took out a handkerchief, mopped his face and exclaimed, "Thank God that's over!" Sheer fear was exuding from his every pore.

Regarding my own visit, I had no such qualms. I was to be met by a charming East German schoolmaster whom I already knew. He spoke perfect English, yet he had never set foot in this country having taught himself English entirely through textbooks. I had in my luggage a book and a few magazines. These were taken out by some East German officials and were put on one side during my passage through Check Point Charlie. Eventually they pretended to read certain passages, turning over the pages in a desultory sort of way. I knew they couldn't read a word of English. They wanted to note my reaction to their examination. Was there anything which might be deemed propaganda? They passed the contents of my suitcase but did not replace my reading matter until I asked for it. There was however no difficulty and I walked on some fifty yards to find my friend waiting for me with a car and a chauffeur.

We had to drive some ten or fifteen miles to an airport hotel, where they had booked a room for me. On the journey I noticed that bunting and flags lined the route. These decorations were not flying from flagpoles but, I suspect for reasons of economy, had been attached to the lamp-posts bordering our route. I asked the cause of their rejoicing and was told that the decorations were in honour of the Hungarian President, who was just departing after a state visit.

At the hotel we were joined by others of their rowing fraternity and sat down to lunch. Suddenly a cannon belched forth from the runway below our window. I asked what it signified. "That, Mr. Neekalls, is the first round of a twenty-one gun salute we are giving in honour of the departure of the Hungarian President." Absentmindedly I counted the reports that followed—seven, eight, nine and then no more—"Only nine," I remarked. "Yes, Mr. Neekalls, we can't understand it." "You know why?" I said. "There's no need to continue, you've shot him down already!" Thank God they didn't take me seriously, for I can't help feeling that, in the particular circumstances, my attempt at humour was a little unwise.

That evening I met the man who had been appointed the East German representative on the Olympic Committee — a charming, soft-spoken man, who a few weeks after his wedding at the beginning of the war had, as a Communist, been confined by Hitler in a concentration camp where he had suffered the most ghastly privations. On the cessation of hostilities he was released — a complete wreck. However it all ended happily, for some five years later his wife gave birth to their first child.

The next morning my schoolmaster guide conducted me to our waiting car and we drove down to the course. Our driver made some remark and his question was passed on to me, "Mr. Neekalls, he wants to know, what 'as 'appened to the Beatles?" I had never realized before to what an extent their fame had penetrated the Iron Curtain. I replied that I had never kept a detailed account of their movements, but that as far as I knew they were all alive and well.

The layout of their rowing course was all that it should be. Their only other visitor from the West was Thomi Keller, the President of the F.I.S.A. During the racing he was kind enough to take me on a launch which had been put at his disposal, and I noted the thoroughness of their preparations in all their various aspects.

Ever since my arrival, whilst driving around, I had noticed a generous sprinkling of coloured men. I was told they were students. Amongst the German officials running the Regatta there was a certain gentleman who seemed to regard me with cynicism. He gave me the impression of being quite unable or unwilling to extend his friendship in my direction. I enquired what he did in private life and was told that he lectured the more advanced students, regardless of race, creed or colour. It put no great strain on my imagination to realize what this almost certainly implied. He was obviously instructing the "more advanced students" how best to throw off the yoke of their imperialist oppressors.

The first evening my hosts staged a very pleasant dinner in honour of Thomi Keller and myself. Mutual laudatory speeches were made and they presented me with some small but remarkably efficient field glasses which was certainly a kindly gesture.

The following day the rowing programme did not start until the afternoon. I was asked if there was anything I would particularly like to do. I said I would like to see the Berlin Wall from their side.

On our way into Berlin, our driver suddenly shouted in excitement what sounded like "Lilac, lilac, lilac". I was obviously under some misapprehension. The flowering lilac, if ever there was any, had faded some months previously. Questioning revealed the fact that our driver had spotted a Leyland lorry—certainly something of a rarity; something moreover that had aroused his enthusiasm.

Arrived at the Wall we visited two manned check points where those with the necessary visas could pass to and from the Western Sector. At each of these outposts they drew my attention to small shrines decorated with flowers and bearing appropriate inscriptions. They were there, I was told, to mark the spot where their sentries had been shot in cold blood by sentries in the Western Sector. They pointed to a flat roof on the far side of the Wall and recounted the following story. One morning they had noticed certain activity on the roof. For some reason the West Germans were positioning a TV camera. In the afternoon their object was revealed when a Western official armed with all the correct passes marched through the Wall, shot their sentry dead and returned unhindered the way he had come. The TV camera had been put there to record this gruesome premeditated episode. In the circumstances I thought it best not to remind them of the thousands of their own countrymen whom they had murdered when spotted trying to escape to a freer environment.

I noticed we were standing on a road with tram lines leading up to the Wall. On the other side stood a skyscraper type of building. I was told that this had been built as offices for one of the big West German newspaper proprietors. The building had been placed there deliberately, so my companions believed, to emphasize that never would anyone from the East ever again use that road. It was blocked once and for all. "How can you be friendly with such people?" they asked.

Next they took me to a block of flats that had been built not long before. Everything, I was to note, was slick, modern and convenient. They then showed me a dreary-looking tenement building which had somehow survived the Russian bombardment. They wished me to notice how things had improved under their aegis. Fancy expecting people to live in such slums, as they obviously had done, prior to their coming. I felt this to be the most blatant piece of propaganda. However, I deemed it best to keep silent. I refrained from mentioning that one could find old, ill-equipped buildings nestling against sleek modern blocks in every town that had suffered war damage. It wasn't a question of new brooms sweeping clean so much as the general advance in planning and building that had ensued since the war.

On my last evening there was a dinner, dancing and the usual junketings invariably associated with the termination of a successful regatta, and the next morning my kind guide deposited me at Check Point Charlie. They looked at such passes and credentials as I possessed, which I imagined were all in order. No, they weren't satisfied. I couldn't pass through. They didn't understand me and I didn't understand them. Luckily someone came to my assistance and I tried to explain my predicament. Still they were not satisfied. I was in a hell of a mess. All my East German rowing acquaintances had gone to their respective homes and I hadn't the slightest idea where I could find them nor, except in one or two instances, did I even know their names. What could I do? I felt a certain inward panic. I ransacked my pockets to try to find something to substantiate my story. I found a letter. What was it? What a bit of luck! It was the original letter from East Germany written weeks before and asking me to be their guest. That did the trick. I was allowed to pass. To say I was relieved would be an understatement. I was sweating.

Postscript

In 1929 I married Rachel Serocold and have had no children—a fact that has never worried me in the least. My wife is an introvert whilst dubbing me a "roaring extrovert". Those opposing factors in our personalities have worked out very well. Her quelling eye has proved a useful brake in my more expansive and noisier moments and has on many occasions saved me, I hope, from a certain self-esteem. On one occasion when I showed signs of being too pleased with myself she declared, "What you need is a jolly good snubbing down." I expect she was right.

In theatre programmes in the past there was often a page entitled "Confessions". One of the questions it posed was, "If not yourself who would you rather be?" My answer has remained constant throughout the years. "If not myself who would I rather be?" Noël Coward. I never met him personally, but I have admired his work, his wit and his mind ever since that evening way back in 1924 when I went to a performance of "The Vortex". Incidentally we were born in the same year. Not long before his death he made a film "This is Noël Coward". The final words he spoke in that film reflect my sentiments to a nicety. I would however qualify one word "successes". In my case it should read "little successes". This is how he finished—"Sum it up? Well, now comes the terrible decision as to whether to be corny or not. The answer is one word. Love. To know that you are among people you love and who love you. This has made all the successes wonderful—much more wonderful than they would have been anyway and I don't think there is any more to be said after that. That's it."

Let me declare at once that I am one of those who steadfastly refuse to admit that the party's over. I believe, and hope I will continue to believe, that there is always a further

POSTSCRIPT

trickle of juice to be squeezed from the orange, however dilapidated its appearance. Should any doubts assail me, I console myself with the thought that the mere fact of the melody lingering on is in itself a great blessing, and in many ways more satisfying than the party itself.

For me, I am glad to record that the melody is happily selective. I remember only the high spots: the sunny days; the successful culmination of some endeavour; the gaiety and love of friends. Conveniently I forget the drear days; the anxieties; the struggles; the ambitions that came to nothing. I just float on in an aura of contentment and gratitude. Thank God for that.

I realize that I am and always have been a privileged person. Nowadays, for some reason, privilege has become a dirty word. I know that I should be thoroughly ashamed of myself for being privileged, but I'm not. I can't see that it is my fault, and anyhow what am I meant to do about it? How does one set out to become normal or underprivileged? What I should have considered blameworthy would have been to have squandered my advantages or used my undoubted blessings to the detriment of others less fortunate than myself. To such an indictment, I plead Not Guilty.

Index

Alexander of Tunis, 136
Alington, Rev. Cyril, 47
Ampthill, Oliver Villiers, 2nd Baron, 144
Arnott, Noel, 132

Bedford, 13th Duke of, 137
Beresford, Jack, 83
Birley, Sir Robert, 37, 44
Bucknall, H. C., 142
Bushell, Anthony, 155, 156

Castéja, Comte de, 38
Church, Tommy, 98
Churchill, Lord Ivor, 80
Churchill, Sir Winston, 60, 86, 121, 135
Clapperton, G. D., 96, 98
Colbert, Mrs., 117
Courtneidge, Cecily, 85

de Havilland, R. S., 41
Desborough, family of, 22
Drinkwater, John, 107

Earl, Sebastian, 129

Fagan, J. B., 84, 85
Fletcher, C. R. L., 42, 77
Fox, Gifford, 113
Fox, Sir Gilbert, 113

Gardiner, Baron of Kittisford, 84
Garton, John, 160
George VI, H.M., 155
Gilbey, W. and A. Ltd., 81, 128
Gold, Sir Harcourt, 170
Graham, Harry, 33
Grenfell, Hon. Billy, 22
Grenfell, Hon. Julian, 22

Grenfell, Hon. Monica, 22

Hallam, Basil, 49, 50
Hampshire, G. K., 139
Harris, Sir Austen, 129, 130, 131
Harris, Peter, 130
Heathcoat-Amory, Sir John, 41
Herrick, Robert F., 101, 103
Hess, Myra, 159
Higginson, General Sir George, 149
Hilary, Richard, 58
Horsfall, E. D., 81, 82
Howes, Bobby, 85
Hulbert, Jack, 85
Huxley, Aldous, 46
Huyse-Eliot, Capt., 62

Isham, Sir Gyles, 86

Jebb, Gladwyn, 1st Baron, 44

Keller, Thomi, 186
Kelly, J. B., 83
Kindersley, Hugh., 2nd Baron, 36

Lampson, Sir Miles, 135
Leger, H. L., 123
Leney, Donald, 36
Leverhulme, 1st Viscount, 113
Lohr, Marie, 96
Lucas, R. C. S., 81, 147, 161, 166, 167

Mallam, Dr. Patrick, 125, 175
Manningham-Buller, Reginald, 1st Baron Dilhorne, 181
Marriott, R. A., 54
Milne, General, 69
Morton, J. B., 110
Mott, Helga, 159

INDEX

Nesbitt, Cathleen, 84
Nichols, Beverley, 86, 87

Page, J. H., 176
Pemberton, Alfred, 118
Pemberton, Max, 118
Pertwee, Roland, 15
Phelps, "Bossy", 148
Philipps, "Cooey", 94
Phillips, Wogan, 2nd Baron Milford, 142
Pitman, C. M. ("Cherry"), 94
Playford, Rev. Humphrey, 98
Powell, Eric, 119

Raikes, D. T., 98, 100, 104
Railston, Col., 63
Ramage, Cecil, 84
Reith, John, 1st Baron, 152
Rickett, Harold, 175
Robey, George, 49

Seagrave, Sir Henry, 146
Shaw, Bishop E., 26
Sieveking, Lance, 154

Sitwell, Sacheverell, 35
Snagge, John, 151, 154, 159, 160
Sparks, Sir Ashley, 106
Squire, Sir John, 151

Talbot, Col. Patrick, 52
Tennyson d'Eyncourt, Patrick, 86
Thackeray, W. M., 13
Trinder, Tommy, 154
Turner, Theo, 129

Urquhart, F. F., 43

Vanden Heuvel, Francis, 117

Wales, Prince of, 86
Warren, Sir Herbert, 79, 87, 93
Watney, Harry, 20
Wilder, Frederick, 21
Wilder, Miss Helen, 21
Wilder, Miss Queenie, 21
Williams, family of, 21
Wimperis, Arthur, 86
Winnington, Ingram, Dr. Arthur Foley, 125